One for
THE GIPPER

One for
THE GIPPER

George Gipp, Knute Rockne, and Notre Dame

Patrick Chelland

Henry Regnery Company • Chicago

Library of Congress Cataloging in Publication Data
Chelland, Patrick, 1928-
    One for the Gipper.
    1. Gipp, George, 1895-   I. Title.
GV939.G53C47   796.33'2'0924 [B]   73-6453

1 2 3 4 5 6 7 ← P Y → 9 8 7 6 5 4 3

Copyright © 1973 by Patrick Chelland. All rights reserved.
Published by Henry Regnery Company
114 West Illinois Street, Chicago, Illinois 60610
Manufactured in the United States of America
Library of Congress Catalog Card Number: 73-6453

To my wife and son

Contents

Sources and Acknowledgments **ix**

1. The Legend **1**
2. The Early Years **15**
3. The Making of a Superstar **28**
4. Gipp Enters Notre Dame **40**
5. A Freshman Phenom **53**
6. Gipp Makes the Varsity **63**
7. Rockne Takes Over **75**
8. The Season That Almost Wasn't **89**
9. From Gridiron Hero to Billiards Star **102**
10. Gipp Clicks—Irish 1919 Western Football Champs **112**
11. Problems of a Superstar **128**
12. A Summer in Flint **140**
13. Gipp's Aerials Bomb Army **154**
14. Short-lived Glory **171**
15. The Last Days **184**
16. Summing Up **194**
    Index **211**

Sources and Acknowledgments

A debt of gratitude is owed to Hunk Anderson, who during the course of compiling material for this book gave generously of his time so that the author might get a clear picture of a period of history long since past. His immense knowledge of football, plus a preternatural ability to recall vividly many of the people, places, and events herein depicted, contributed greatly to this work.

A debt of gratitude also is owed to the following, who gave of their time freely and unselfishly, often above and beyond the call of duty: Elizabeth Dales at the South Bend Public Library; Charles Stetter, Principal of Calumet High School; Archie R. Campbell; Ed Tobola; Mrs. Dorothy Gipp Taylor; Mrs. Manilla Gipp; and Anna Hogan.

Grateful acknowledgment is extended to all those at the University of Notre Dame who willingly assisted the author in this project. Special thanks to the following Gipp football

ix

teammates: Leonard Bahan, Walter Miller, Roger Kiley, Norman Barry, Harry Mehre, Donald Grant, Frank Rydzewski, Lawrence Shaw, Maurice Smith, Edward Anderson, and Arthur Bergman.

Others who deserve mention are as follows: Mrs. Mary Ann Homer, Flint Public Library; Eugene H. Burrell, Elkhart Public Library; Mrs. Florence Mote, Indiana State Library; Irene Mischler, Indianapolis Public Library; Ruth Kell, Peter White Public Library, Marquette, Michigan; A. Day, Gilbert M. Simmons Library, Kenosha, Wisconsin; Michigan Technological University Library; Winifred Cosbey, Elkhart County Historical Society; Mrs. Nadine Whelchel, Federal Records Center; Mrs. Bernadette Church, Morrison Waite High School, Toledo, Ohio; Mrs. Kathleen Johnson, Librarian, St. Vincent Hospital, Sioux City, Iowa; The National Archives, Washington, D.C.; W. J. Mills, Indiana Bell Telephone; Frank Baumgarten, Saginaw Bell Telephone; Dennis R. Bodem, State Archivist, Michigan Department of State; Margaret Stukel, Clerk, Village of Calumet; Calumet Public Library; Houghton Historical Society; Wm. J. Kilkenny, Knox College; Bennie Osterbaum, University of Michigan; Mrs. Hazen Cuyler; Mrs. Hugo Otopalik; Mildred Osborne; William Ellis; Clarke Pittenger; William Bruggner; Ernie Vick; Geraldine Gipp; Mrs. Ann Barrett; Mrs. Charles Hart; Mrs. Natalie Hays; George G. Metten; Jerry Pfarr; Mrs. Claire Scott; and Mrs. Bertha Honold.

Also Charles Shriver, Chicago Cubs Baseball Team; Garry Schumacher, San Francisco Giants Baseball Team; Glen R. Rasmussen, Dean, Morningside College; Chancellor Mark Hobson, University of Nebraska; Fred W. Stabley, Michigan State University; Walter Paulison, Northwestern University; Duane Purvis, Purdue University; Bud Brown, University of South Dakota; Alan Anderson, Morningside College; Don

Bryant, University of Nebraska; Emory Bauer and John Krause, Valparaiso University; Gerald Dreyer, Wabash College; Hal Bateman, Western Michigan University; Frank Walter and M. Salvani of the United States Military Academy; Mrs. Eilene Gresham, Case Western Reserve University; Van Glendale, Indiana University; Russell Rice, University of Kentucky; and the publicity departments of Mount Union and Kalamazoo Colleges.

Newspapers and Magazines

Daily Mining Gazette; Flint Journal; South Bend Tribune; South Bend Times; Marquette Daily Mining Journal; Keweenaw Miner; Indianapolis Star; Collier's Magazine

Books

American Military History. Department of the Army, 1956.

Beach, Jim. *Notre Dame Football.* New York: MacFadden-Bartell, 1962.

Grant, Chet. *Before Rockne at Notre Dame.* South Bend: Dujarie Press, 1969.

Murdoch, Angus. *Boom Copper,* 1943.

Rice, Grantland. *The Tumult and the Shouting.* New York: A.S. Barnes, 1954.

Stuhldreher, Harry A. *Knute Rockne, Man Builder.* Philadelphia: MacRae Smith, 1931.

1.

The Legend

GEORGE Gipp was the first Notre Dame football player to win top All-American honors. He achieved this extraordinary feat in 1920 when Walter Camp, the father of American football, selected George as the fullback on his All-American eleven. Until then, the best Notre Dame had been able to do was occasionally to place one of its stars on a Camp second team. What makes Gipp's accomplishment all the more remarkable is that it came at a time when Notre Dame was nothing more than a small, relatively obscure Midwestern college, a time when intercollegiate football, born in the East and primarily an Eastern sport, looked to the larger Eastern universities for nearly all of the manpower for the more prestigious All-American teams. Nowhere was this more evident than in Camp's yearly selections; by far the most prestigious and publicized of all existing All-American teams, his were stacked with stars from such schools as Yale,

1

Princeton, Harvard, Penn, Rutgers, and West Point. George Gipp put an end to such provincial preference and in so doing opened the way for future non-Eastern players, including those who were to follow him at South Bend.

In its long tradition of winning football, Notre Dame has produced more gridiron superstars than has any other college or university in the country—Louis Salmon, M. Harry Miller, Harry Stuhldreher, Jim Crowley, Bill Shakespeare, Angelo Bertelli, Bob Williams, and Nick Eddy, to name just a few—but none of these men was able to attain the same universal, perdurable fame as Gipp.

The reasons for this are manifold: Gipp was one of the first of that rare breed of player that has since come to be known as the triple-threat, and he was one of the last of that equally rare breed capable, because of superior skills in both the offensive and defensive departments of the game, of going a full sixty minutes. Everything he did on the field was near perfection, and though he was never known to underestimate an opponent, he was seldom averse to taking a wild gamble in a tight game if he felt that it might just produce victory.

Gipp's gridiron exploits kept him in the national spotlight throughout his collegiate career. He began as a freshman with his dramatic, game-winning 62-yard drop kick (still the second longest in intercollegiate competition) and ending with his game-winning touchdown against an upset-minded Indiana eleven only minutes after returning to action late in the final quarter, writhing from the pain of a severely separated right shoulder sustained during the early minutes of the first quarter.

In between, in a career that spanned close to four full years of varsity performance, he had done so many daring things with a pigskin that the fans had elevated him to the rank of a demigod. Gipp enjoyed a position of prominence comparable to that of such celebrities of the day as Woodrow Wilson, John Pershing, Enrico Caruso, and Charlie Chaplin. Then, at the pinnacle of his career, Gipp suddenly became gravely ill. A nation accustomed to heralding his gridiron feats found itself genuinely concerned, offering up earnest prayers for his eventual recovery.

There can be little doubt that George's untimely death helped to broaden and perpetuate the Gipp legend. Nor can there be doubt as to the sizable contribution afforded the legend by George himself when, on his deathbed, he supposedly thought not of himself but of his alma mater, entreating Coach Rockne to request some future Notre Dame team, when fighting a losing battle, to go out and "win one for the Gipper." Although there is no evidence to corroborate or refute this final request of Gipp's, it did have a devastating effect on the general public in later years and on the mediocre Notre Dame team that represented the school nearly a decade after Gipp's death.

It was not until 1928 that Coach Rockne decided the time was right to make known Gipp's final request. Rockne delivered it with dramatic impact in the locker room during half-time against a fine West Point team. This scene, recreated by Pat O'Brien in the film version of Knute Rockne's life, became the high point of the movie. Who could forget that touching locker-room scene, or the battered and bruised face of Jack Chevigny as he smashed his way through a formidable Army line for the game-winning touchdown? And who could forget his choked words as he slowly pulled himself back up: "That's one for the Gipper." The movie succeeded in introducing a whole new generation to the greatness that was George Gipp's, and almost overnight his name became a household word. Even in homes whose occupants had never seen a football, the name George Gipp was to ring an instant bell.

George Gipp had all the necessary equipment to become a star. He was six feet two and weighed in at a solid 186 pounds, which Coach Rockne described as "all bone and muscle." He was incredibly quick and well-coordinated and moved on long, sturdy legs with a seemingly poetic grace.

Gipp was one of the best passers of his day. He threw what can best be described as a lob pass, the only pass then feasible since the football was somewhat stubbier than the one in use today. The ball was difficult to grip, and a passer had to let the ball slide off his palm and depend almost solely on good wrist action and a powerful arm to insure accuracy and distance. Gipp found the matter relatively simple. He could throw a pass fifty yards or more with the accuracy of a sharpshooter blasting away at clay pigeons. And according to Roger Kiley, on the receiving end of many a Gipp pass, they were "light as a feather."

As a runner Gipp combined the speed and power of a Bengal tiger; he was able to run the 100 in 10.2 seconds in full football dress. When he smashed into the line on his favorite off-tackle play, tacklers found him almost impossible to haul down. Often it took several determined opponents to accomplish this feat. So swift was his acceleration once he received the snap from center that he was often well past the secondary before anybody could get a hand on any part of his body. His broken field running, according to Roger Kiley, was a thing of beauty: "the long stride, weaving, changing direction, so very graceful."

Gipp's punts were usually low and slightly arched in their trajectory, like a line drive in baseball, and they ranged forty yards and beyond in actual flight. But his real forte was drop kicking. He seems to have mastered this tricky art with the ease with which a newborn colt learns to stand up and walk just minutes after its birth. To find Gipp's equal in drop kicking one would have to go back to Jim Thorpe.

Unfortunately, the period around World War I to which Gipp belonged makes it difficult to confirm the legend. There was no television, and radio was just then coming into its own. Movie cameras were extant, but nobody seems to have recorded Gipp on film. In fact, still photos of him are a rarity —Gipp disliked posing for a portrait. Much worse than the absence of either films or photos, however, is our lack of even one Gipp interview by either a newspaper or leading magazine of the day. Evidently no reporter had the foresight to trap Gipp and record what surely would have been a priceless interview. Therefore, we are devoid of his personal observations, comments, and recollections.

All we really know about Gipp has been handed down to us from local newspapers and the sketchy observations of friends, teammates, and casual acquaintances. Even his gridiron accomplishments, limited to newspaper coverage of the day, are sadly lacking in detail. In Gipp's time only the greenest of reporters were assigned to cover athletic events, and so their accounts are in most cases relatively sparse and poorly written. In fact, in the Midwest at least, first names of athletes were seldom printed. So any authoritative description of Gipp as a performer finally has to come from the handful of coaches, players, fans, and reliable newspapermen who were privileged to see George in action. Surprisingly, only a total of one hundred thousand fans had the pleasure of watching him play.

One of the major reporters of the day privileged to have seen a Gipp performance was Grantland Rice, the acknowledged dean of American sportswriters. Grant, as he was known to his closest friends, happened to be in the stands on that cold, clear October day in 1920 when George put on one of the greatest gridiron shows of all time. All afternoon he electrified some ten thousand fans with a display of passing, kicking, and broken field running the likes of which had never been seen at West Point. When it was over, when he left the game for a substitute in the closing moments, bloody-

faced and battered, those grateful fans showed their appreciation by rising in silent tribute. So impressed was he by what
he had seen that Rice, some thirty years later in a book published shortly before his death, chose George Gipp as left
halfback for his all-time college eleven. Quite an honor, coming from a man who had seen them all in over fifty years of
covering collegiate football.

Another celebrity of the day who saw Gipp in action, and
more than once, was the celebrated author Ring Lardner. A
loyal rooter for Notre Dame throughout his life, Lardner
served his apprenticeship covering the sports scene in South
Bend some years before Gipp's arrival there. At mid-season
in 1918 Lardner wrote of Gipp: "Notre Dame has one signal:
pass the ball to Gipp and let him use his own judgment."

Lardner's admiration for Gipp was shared by perhaps the
greatest coach ever produced in the collegiate ranks—the immortal Knute Rockne. In an article written for *Collier's*
magazine nearly a decade after the death of his star, Rockne
put down some impressive comments on why he held Gipp to
be the greatest football player who ever lived—and remember
that Rockne had both seen and played against Jim Thorpe
at the height of both his collegiate and professional careers.
In explaining Gipp's greatness, Rockne wrote: "He was a
natural athlete. And he possessed the three most important
qualities needed to attain greatness: the qualities of body,
mind, and spirit. He had what no coach or system can teach
—football intuition."

Rockne illustrated Gipp's intuition by recalling the Army
game of 1917. "We had Army beaten 7-2 as we came to the
last minutes of play. The Cadets marched for several first
downs, planting the ball down on our 20-yard line. There
they were held, but advanced for the fourth and final down
to our 8-yard line. Remember the score was 7-2. Gipp
remembered it. Army's quarterback barked signals and they

lined up for a place kick. Gipp instantly cried: 'Look out for
a pass!' He was right. Army did not kick. They went for six
points instead of an almost certain three. Six points would
have won the game, but Gipp warned our defense in time.
Receivers were covered, and he himself knocked down the
pass and saved the game."

Another Gipp attribute that impressed Rockne was his
quick wit and great sense of humor. The legendary Irish mentor gave the example of the grueling late-season encounter
with Purdue in 1919. "Early in the game Gipp broke away for
a tremendous long run, only to have the play called back
by an alert official who cited an infraction and penalized us
5 yards. On the very next play Gipp again broke away for
an even longer gain—80 yards, to be exact. Again the same
referee, on the alert for infractions, called the play back and
penalized us another 5 yards. Chagrined, Gipp stomped over
to the referee: 'Next time blow the whistle once for me to
start and twice for me to stop!'"

Rockne, aside from being the very best at his job, was a
born actor. He loved the dramatics associated with the game
almost as much as he loved the game itself. And maybe this,
too, was one of the reasons he became so attached to his first
great star. In Gipp he saw something of himself, the true
lover of the dramatic and a bit of the showman. "The high
dramatic moments of the major battles found him daring,
hard-hitting, almost vicious in his attack," Rockne said of
Gipp, "and no matter how feverishly eager he appeared, he
was always internally cold. The boy was really a master
showman, with the alert mind to catch every effective detail
of a show. Secretly, although he gave no outward sign, he
loved the dramatic." For all intents and purposes Rockne
could have been talking about himself.

Whenever the name of Gipp is mentioned in sport circles
the conversation concerns his great passing, kicking, and run-

ning, and because of these highly publicized qualities, his brilliant defensive qualities have been sadly overshadowed. The truth is that Gipp was every bit as good on defense as he was on offense. He was able in his years at Notre Dame to reduce even that technique to an exact science. For one thing, he seldom openly tackled a man; he preferred, with the cunning and skill of a trained sheep dog herding one of its sheep into a desired place, to force the ball carrier to the side lines, thus avoiding what he called useless body contact. But when there was no other recourse, his tackles were vicious and deadly, and according to Rockne, it could truly be said that there was never a pass completed in territory patrolled by Gipp.

On the field George was the quintessence of determination and self-confidence, knowing instinctively just what was required of him and always able to do just that. But off the field was another matter entirely. He seems to have been a confused young man, often uncertain as to the course in which he wished to travel. In the beginning he was a liberal arts student at Notre Dame; then quite suddenly he changed his major to law. Nobody seems to have known why. In any case, he was uncertain as to whether or not he would graduate law school and just as undecided as to whether he really wanted to be a practicing attorney.

The contradictions Gipp held within him are enough to stagger one's imagination. He was a quiet, laconic young man who seemed to rejoice in the privacy of his own company, yet he could thrive in the noisy, gregarious atmosphere of the pool and poker halls that became his favorite haunts shortly after arriving in South Bend. Women were attracted to him because of his fame and his manly good looks, and at the height of his career he merely had to whistle to get the girl of his choice. Yet he seems to have had little desire for the role of Don Juan. When he finally fell in love, he picked a girl who was bad for him, and she broke his heart. Rockne said Gipp was dramatic and a bit of a showman, and there can be no doubt of this; yet he seems to have found no joy in the publicity his performances on the field produced. Never once did he read a newspaper piece in which his name appeared.

That he was a complex man there can be little doubt. Personal recollections of him are so clouded by contradictions that a true determination of his character seems to be an almost impossible task. Some people who claim to have known him intimately have called him selfish and self-indulgent; others, who claim to have known him equally as well, found him to be sincere, altruistic, and generous almost to a fault. Some have called him a sociable, well-mannered young man whose basic charm lay in a childlike proclivity to shyness. Still others, obdurate in their dislike, have denounced him as being aloof and egocentric, often displaying a calculating approach to friendship.

There was only one point on which those who knew Gipp seem to have agreed, that being his good looks. All agree he fit perfectly the image that comes to mind the minute the word "hero" is mentioned. Aside from his height and near-perfect body symmetry, he had a handsomeness that is often mentioned by the women who recall Gipp. They remember the straight, dark-brown hair, the wide forehead, the stern, well-molded chin, and the generous mouth that was apt to break into a sudden boyish grin at the slightest provocation. But mostly they recall the large, gentle blue eyes that many swear held an ever-present hint of some distant melancholy.

It is not generally known that George Gipp did not come to Notre Dame to play football; rather, he came on a baseball scholarship. This is not really surprising, and for two good reasons. When George Gipp came to Notre Dame, baseball was the school's major sport, the one that brought the school the modicum of attention it enjoyed at this time in regions beyond the Midwest, particularly the East coast. Something like twenty of Notre Dame's alumni had gone on to outstanding careers in the major leagues, including the celebrated Adrian "Cap" Anson. Secondly, Gipp was capable of becoming perhaps the greatest player ever to come out of the South Bend school. He could hit, field, and run the bases with the skill of one of the great stars of his day, Tyrus Raymond Cobb. On the amateur diamonds of his home town they did, in fact, call him the next Ty Cobb. Unlike Cobb, however, he packed a Ruthian wallop, and several of his home runs hit in crucial games are still remembered as the longest ever hit in his home area. Gipp had a great arm, also, probably coming closest to the Yankee Clipper, Joe DiMaggio, in distance and power. His brilliant glove work as a center fielder often was compared to that of another great defensive star of his day, Tris Speaker.

"Baseball's my game," Gipp reportedly informed Rockne on their first encounter. But George was being a bit too modest, for he should have added, "and basketball, too."

Although he did not play nearly as much basketball as he did baseball or football, Gipp was nevertheless an outstanding court performer. At Notre Dame he forsook the sport and played only a handful of games, probably because at the time basketball was not as rewarding a sport in intercollegiate circles as was football or baseball; yet he played long enough to impress Roger Kiley, himself a better than average cage performer, with his versatility. Kiley recalled that "George was the first player I ever saw shoot a basket with one hand." Back home people were much more elaborate in describing Gipp's basketball prowess, recalling in detail how as a high school freshman he led his team to twenty-four wins in one season and a regional championship. Later his brilliant play in a tournament brought his local YMCA its first basketball trophy.

Sports was Gipp's main interest, and baseball was his first love. His major vice was gambling, which he relished. He learned to shoot pool at the local YMCA, and by the time he was sixteen he was able to earn all the spending money he needed by betting on himself. After running out of suitable competition in pocket billiards, George turned to the more difficult art of three-cushion billiards. He proceeded to master this with the same ease he seems to have mastered everything else he tried.

Not all of Gipp's winnings came from pool, however. A sizable portion came from playing poker. He was one of those young men who find nothing wrong in staying up all night playing cards, especially when he would walk home in the bright morning sun counting his winnings. A local mining official in his home town said of Gipp, "That sonofabitch knows every card you got in your hand."

Unfortunately, the diligence Gipp displayed in games of chance never fully manifested itself in his academic life. During his high school days he frequently was absent from class, but he did get to school often enough to gain a reputation as a loafer, class wit, and incorrigible disrupter of classroom harmony, plus the added notoriety of being a master prankster. It was like Tom Sawyer coming to life.

While at Notre Dame Gipp was forever fighting an almost uncontrollable urge to quit school. A born nonconformist, he never could get fully accustomed to the imposed routine of student life, and there was something about the order of it all that filled him with a sense of uneasiness. Like a Shakespearian actor forced to accept a role he considered beneath his dignity, Gipp often played his role quite badly.

Much of the unfavorable criticism leveled against Gipp in recent years stems from his apparent lack of self-discipline. Many modern writers in attempting to probe the Gipp mystique have been able to find little else with which to discredit the man, and possibly for this reason alone they have blown Gipp's discipline problems well out of proportion. They have gone about their work unmercifully; Gipp emerges as a vain, selfish prima donna in some accounts, and in others he is branded as a shameless hedonist who, in an unceasing search for self-gratification, broke all of the rules of good conduct, especially those that pertain to a national celebrity. In breaking some of these rules, Gipp's critics contend, he was instrumental in undermining his team's morale.

Gipp's detractors also contend that his all-night pool and poker extravaganzas, especially on the eve of an important game, cut a sizable swath out of his playing proficiency the next day. Harry Stuhldreher, in a book written shortly after the tragic death of Knute Rockne, said that Gipp "appeared sometimes to be lazy and indifferent on the playing field, but only because at the time Notre Dame was playing an opponent far below the par to which it had become accustomed. And had Notre Dame played only inferior opponents, chances are nobody would have ever heard of George Gipp." Detractors of Gipp have taken Stuhldreher's words out of context and claimed that because of his lack of self-discipline, Gipp abused his body fiercely, that his seemingly lazy and indifferent attitude was, in reality, the outward sign of atrophy in the body of a very tired young man. However, George Gipp's accomplishments at Notre Dame do not bear out any of these allegations. Concerning his efficiency on the field, let the record speak for itself: disregarding the final five games of the 1917 season, which George missed due to a leg injury, he did not miss a game on the Notre Dame schedule for three years, save the final one against Michigan A&M. During that game he was confined to a hospital bed. Concerning his performance during those years, Gipp was able to compile a total offense record that was good enough to stand for nearly a half century—hardly the record of a prima donna performing with a body worn to the breaking point by overindulgence in life's pleasures.

A half century has passed since George Gipp, the greatest of all the Notre Dame stars, played his last game. But still he haunts us. Just the mention of "the Gipper" is enough to stir the most somnolent of human imaginations. And one is sometimes moved to ask why. Why, after some fifty years and hundreds of succeeding stars, is one man still able to stir so much emotion? Perhaps the answer lies not only in the man but also in the particular time in which his star shone. We must remember that Gipp came along at a perfect time, that unique era we call the "Innocent Years," and he stayed on just long enough to usher in that most dazzling of all American eras, the "Roaring Twenties," known to sports buffs as the "Golden Age of Sports."

It was a great time to have lived, a time when a cocky America, exulting in its new-found power, was progressing far beyond its wildest imaginings. Its people seemed to bristle with enthusiasm. Everything seemed new and fresh, daring and exciting, and anywhere one looked there was something that had to be done, some challenge to be met. There always seemed to be someone around to get things done, and the people immediately crowned that someone a hero. Americans seemed to have had an uncanny knack for converting extraordinary men into heroes, and when they weren't crowning heroes they went about creating them. It was the only era in which Frank Merriwell of Yale could have been born into the world of fiction. It was the era that craved and loved its heroes, and its symbol was George Gipp.

It was a time, too, that foreshadowed a future of agonizing complexity while rejoicing in the rare splendor of its own simplicity. There was no television and little radio with which to clutter men's minds. Black was black and white was white and nobody seemed to care much about the hues in between. It was a world of gay abandon in which the individual and not his creation was undisputed ruler, a period marked by romanticism. Today, in a world in which technology has become master and the individual has become a blob of information on computer tape, we sometimes seem to have nothing left but the pleasure of looking back and seeing ourselves as we once were, and how wonderfully simple life had been. And we see, too, George Gipp, standing as tall as a mountain peak and as big as life itself, superior to anything we've created or yet may create for all of our technology. Maybe that is why George Gipp, or, if you prefer, "the Gipper," has the power to move us even today.

2.

The Early Years

THE northernmost part of Michigan's Upper Peninsula is a slightly crooked, tapering piece of land that begins at the mainland and culminates some fifty-six miles later at the sandy brim of the greatest body of fresh water in the world, Lake Superior. The peninsula is bordered on the east, west, and north by the lake and is therefore a helpless victim of the lake's merciless winter winds. This frigid piece of property is called the Keweenaw Peninsula. Sightseers and scientists consider it to be a quirk of nature for two distinct reasons.

The first, and more obvious, one is its topography. Unlike the Middle West, with its great expanse of low, flat farmland that in the bloom of summer seems to exult in its endless acres of wheat, oats, barley, and corn, the Keweenaw is a sunburst of spectacular scenery. Its wild cliffs and crags, where cedar and tamarack trees grow in great profusion, and its swampy

15

terrain camouflaged by a thin cushion of soft pine look, as its most noted historian observed, "like a part of the Maine coastline transplanted intact to the Middle West, or a piece of Colorado misplaced to the east."

The second unusual aspect of the Keweenaw, and the one that confounds geologists, concerns what once lay beneath its pine rug. Just a century ago the Keweenaw Peninsula contained the first and richest deposits of native copper to be found anywhere in the world. The Keweenaw became the site of the first mining boom in North America, coming some six years before the great Sutter gold strike in California. Thousands of voracious Easterners swarmed over the land as a flock of vultures swarms over a dried carcass. By the time copper mining in the Keweenaw finally had run its course, some 8.5 billion pounds of the red metal had been extracted from the earth and upwards of one hundred thousand men had earned their living from this vast enterprise. At the height of production there were thrity-one different nationalities represented in the Keweenaw, coming from half the countries of the world. The first to come were the Cornishmen, or "Cousin Jacks" as they were known, from Cornwall, England. They soon were followed by the Scandinavians: first the Swedes, then the Norwegians and the Danes. Then came the Finns, the Irish, Poles, Italians, Chinese, and Germans.

George Gipp's paternal ancestors were German. His grandfather, Antoine Gipp, born in Lutzrath, Prussia in 1820, was the first of the family to come to America, being part of the great influx of political refugees who fled their native land during the abortive revolution of 1848. He brought with him his pretty young wife, the former Agnes Beltes, whom he had met and married the previous year. Originally, the Gipps settled in Albany, New York, and it was there that the elder Gipp learned his trade as a plasterer and stone mason. It was there, too, that three of the Gipps' six children were born: Mary, Matthew, and John.

After reading a banner story carried by nearly all of the Eastern newspapers concerning the accidental discovery of copper in Michigan, Antoine Gipp knew that here was the place he wished to settle. But it was to take four years of waiting to realize his dream. In 1857, when the family had put aside sufficient money toward rail fare, Antoine gathered together his meager belongings, packed them in a trunk, and put his family on a train that was westward bound.

The Gipps settled on a long tract of land that was the property of the local mining company, situated between Calumet and what was to be the village of Laurium. It was at this site and while living in a company-owned house that the last of the Gipp children were born: Lizzie, Kate, and Louis. During those years in their new surroundings, Antoine Gipp worked as a laborer for the local mining company, which was to become in the next decade as impressive a force in the copper mining industry as its name implied: the Calumet and Heckla Consolidated Copper Mining Company. The company was such an integral part of the Keweenaw and had such a great effect on the times and environment to which George Gipp belonged that a brief history of it seems in order.

After the first copper strike turned out to be a complete bust, ending in disillusionment and poverty for the rush of fortune hunters strewn about the Keweenaw, a search for the precious red metal was abandoned for nearly ten years. In 1853 Ed Hulbert, a handsome young engineer of only twenty, accidentally discovered a mineral he was certain was copper. After locating its source, he hastily purchased 200 acres of land in the vicinity. Because of a lack of money, however, he could only set up a small-scale mining operation that he would carry on for almost a decade. Finally, he was put in contact with the most proper of proper Bostonians, one Quincy Adams Shaw. Shaw advanced the necessary cash, and on September 17, 1864, the great Calumet conglomerate lode was discovered and the Calumet Mining Company officially came into being. Later, with the merger of the Heckla Mining Company, the corporation became the Calumet and Heckla Consolidated Copper Mining Company, which was destined to deliver millions of dollars in profits to its shareholders while gaining world-wide recognition.

The merger of the Calumet and Heckla Mining Companies was less than two years away when, in 1862, Antoine Gipp, aware of the war that raged between the states of his adopted homeland and wanting to do his part, trudged over to Eagle River on a blistering hot day in late August to enlist in the Union Army. He was then forty-two years of age. The following October he was mustered in at Port Huron and assigned to Company C of the 27th Infantry, Michigan Volunteers. He was one of the effectives in Brigadier General Solomon Meredith's gallant Iron Brigade, which had distinguished itself at Gettysburg in the summer of 1863. Later, on May 12, 1864, Gipp received a severe wound of the right arm in the fierce first day's fight at Spotsylvania in Virginia. He was discharged at Delaney House, Washington, D. C., on July 26, 1865, just five days after having been promoted to the rank of sergeant.

The tenure of service of George's grandfather in the Union Army imposed untold financial hardships on his family, and eventually the family was compelled to break up until the end of the hostilities or until such time as Gipp would be able to return home and resume his occupation with the Calumet and Heckla. During this uncertain period the girls, Mary, Lizzie, and Kate, along with the youngest of the brood, Louis, remained at home with their mother, while the two oldest boys, Matthew and John, were adopted temporarily by a family who resided in the nearby village of Eagle River.

Matthew Gipp, the second of Antoine and Agnes Gipp's children, born in 1854, reached young manhood at the time the Calumet and Heckla was in full bloom, its peak period of prosperity beginning in 1870 and ending somewhere in the late 1890's. During these years the C&H became an integral part of life in the Keweenaw. Nowhere in the Peninsula was the gentle hand of the C&H not in evidence. It owned nearly all of the land, and on this property it built twelve hundred liver-colored homes. Employees were encouraged to move in, paying between six and eight dollars a month in rent, depending on the number of bedrooms. The homes were heated by coal brought in by company boats and lighted by company-made electric power. Even the garbage was carted off by horse-drawn company wagons. The copper company was the first major business enterprise in North America to provide a company hospital for its employees and members of their families, and it was the first company to maintain an employee benefit fund to cover sickness and death. The C&H even had a benevolent tentacle on the public school chain; as a result the schools were the best anywhere, and the teachers were the highest paid in the country. Long before it had been accepted by school systems in larger cities, the Froebel system of kindergarten teaching was in use in the Keweenaw public schools.

By the time young Matthew Gipp was ready to seek employment, the C&H offered additional inducements impossible to ignore, the major one being a weekly salary well above the average national scale. Matthew went on the payroll as a carpenter, and later he was to change his occupation to that of a sawyer.

Matthew, who had stayed on in Eagle River, left his adopted family and settled in the section of Calumet that was later to become Laurium but was then the business district of the area. The residents of that village remember him as a handsome young man, standing about five feet eight and weighing 130 pounds. His fair complexion was made striking by a generous mop of auburn hair and a neatly trimmed Vandyke beard. Friends recall him as a quiet, modest man with firm religious convictions.

On June 16, 1877, Matthew Gipp married Isabella Taylor,

the plump, pretty, blue-eyed daughter of a local resident. The couple was married by a Baptist clergyman in Laurium. Isabella came from fine Scotch-Irish stock whose ancestry could be traced back to Northern Ireland. Her father, Alexander Taylor, earned his livelihood for a time tilling the fertile Irish soil and then emigrated to America at approximately the same time as the elder Gipp.

In 1845, shortly after marrying Catherine McInerne, the soft-spoken daughter of a neighboring farmer, Alexander Taylor had escaped the great potato famine that spread across Ireland and took his young wife to the inviting shores of North America. The Taylors settled in New Bedford, Massachusetts, where all four of their children were born. As near as can be determined, the Taylors arrived in the Keweenaw at about the same time as the Gipps.

The marriage of Matthew Gipp and Isabella Taylor, as recounted by those who still have vivid impressions of the pair, was for the most part blissful. Matthew was a hardworking man and, until ill health forced his retirement, a good provider. He was a stern disciplinarian with a zealot's passion for his religious beliefs. Isabella was a gentle woman hardly ever given to outbursts of temper. And she was in her own quiet way a deeply religious woman, belonging to the town's Congregational church. She is best remembered by residents as a sincere, modest woman whose later life was troubled by ill health.

The Gipps gave birth to eight children: Alexander, Matthew, John, Louise, Mary, Bertha, George, and Dorothy. Before any of the children were born, however, Matthew built the modest, two-story, white clapboard house at 432 Heckla Street. It was at this site that on February 18, 1895, George was born to the Gipp family.

There was nothing about the noisy infant that set him apart from any other normal baby. Nor was there anything about him that gave so much as a hint as to the remarkable talents that lay dormant within him. His baby sister Dorothy, whom the family affectionately referred to as Dolly, recalls instead a typical childish quality: "He loved sweets of all sorts."

The neighbors, on the other hand, recall that George did not bear even the slightest resemblance to his two living brothers or to his father. Even as a child his long, gangling frame gave evidence that he was destined to surpass all members of his family in height. From his father he derived his quiet, laconic manner. From his mother he inherited a gentle self-assurance and equanimity of temper. From her, too, he got his dark brown hair and large blue eyes.

Where George's athletic talent came from is anybody's guess. His father was not in the least athletically inclined, nor is there any evidence that any member of the Taylor clan excelled in athletics. Of George's brothers only Matthew, Jr., distinguished himself as an athlete. Young Matt gained a local reputation as a racer in hockey arenas in and around Laurium. In a most peculiar contest, young Matt would challenge any member of opposing hockey teams to a foot race against him. The race was limited to the length of the ice field; the peculiarity was that the hockey player wore his skates and young Matt wore spiked shoes. Matt won most of the races in which he participated.

George was tall for a boy of seven when he entered the Horace Mann Elementary School, and he had the unenviable distinction of being the tallest in his class. Although he was lean and gangly, he was strikingly handsome even then. In his fifth year he transferred to the John Duncan School, where he remained until his transfer to the junior high school located in nearby Calumet.

It was during his years at Calumet Junior High that George's complete indifference to school fully manifested itself. He was a bright boy, but his grades in all subjects were always poor. A lazy, shiftless student, George seemed to despise the hours he was compelled to spend in the classroom. He had an intense aversion to homework and, as a result, almost always came to class unprepared. Teachers marvelled at his keen mind yet were driven to fits of despair by his unwillingness to apply himself. He often was reprimanded for poor penmanship, for example, and in response he took great pains to increase its illegibility.

As early as age fourteen, George already showed signs of nonconformity. Obstinate, unruly, and nearly always in opposition to his superiors, his prime purpose for attending school seemed to be to annoy and frustrate the Establishment. Some classmates remember his quick wit, which became the tool he used to destroy the intense, solemn atmosphere of the classroom. Often a careless, witty remark brought normal class functions to an abrupt halt, and, like the true comedian, George seemed to rejoice in the spontaneous laughter his witticisms produced. In truth he had a passion for unbridled freedom, and humor was his way of punishing the Establishment for the imposition of daily hours of captivity.

Frederic Larson, a classmate of George's at Calumet High and later his roommate for a time at Notre Dame, remembers the frustration George endured as a student. "He reminded me of a young stallion that would rear up, pull back, and then go forward, moving from side to side, all because it disliked anything that looked like it would restrict its freedom. George hated to be restricted. He also could be exceedingly witty. He always had a ready response for any situation. He had difficulty staying in school long enough to compete in sports because the school authorities often expelled him for some prank or sharp remark he would make to one of the teachers. Once I felt the brunt of a Gipp remark myself. It was in our geometry class at Calumet High. I do not recall the question asked me by our teacher; I only recall answering that the figure in question was an isosceles triangle. Suddenly I heard George let out a roar of laughter, and as I stood beside my desk, actually cringing from embarrassment, George said loudly: 'It's the right answer, Fred, but not for that question.'"

George was much the same boy outside the classroom as he was inside it—the perfect young imp, almost always mixed up in some kind of mischief. Fortunately, all of his pranks were harmless in nature. Childhood friends have supplied us with a number of examples of these pranks that help to illustrate young George's nature.

One of his school friends remembers a story that had as its root the Eggen and Hoyems Swedish Bake Shop located on Heckla Street, a few doors down from the Gipp residence. The owners of the shop had hauled out several dozen cases of eggs and stacked them alongside the building. Along came George wearing a heavy corduroy jacket with deep pockets. Spotting the eggs, he sauntered over, broke open one of the crates, and carefully filled his pockets. Then he walked along Heckla Street, stopped everybody he knew, and engaged them in idle conversation. As they chatted, George surreptitiously slipped an egg into each friend's pocket. Then, abruptly terminating the conversation, he slapped the person in the area of the deposited egg. George counted twelve victims in less than an hour.

Another of Gipp's early friends was a boy by the name of Alger Train, whose family was a back-fence neighbor of the Gipps. Alger, several years older than George, worked part-time as maintenance man at the local YMCA, one of George's favorite haunts practically from the time he learned to walk. "Next to the indoor pool," Alger recalled, "there were a number of bathtubs, each partitioned off to afford privacy for the user. In those days all of the businessmen of the town used the YMCA's facilities, including the bathtubs and shower rooms. Every Saturday afternoon a sign painter by the name of Eieth took his bath there. He was a pleasant man, quiet and very modest. On this particular Saturday I was washing windows, and I was drawing my water from a faucet in one of the tub rooms. I didn't see Eieth come in.

"Sometime later, when I went back to get another bucket of clean water, I noticed the door to the tub room I was using was closed. George Gipp and four other boys were standing in front of the door, and, seeing me hesitate momentarily in front of it, George said, 'It's okay, Alger, go ahead in—nobody's in there.' So I walked in. No sooner was I inside when I felt the excruciating pain that comes from being struck in the head with a hard object. I fell backwards, slightly dazed, and heard an angry voice cry out, 'Get the hell out and stay out!' Later I learned that George had seen Eieth go into the tub room. He gathered his friends together, and they proceeded to take turns opening the door on the man as he sat in his tub. Pretending surprise at finding someone occupying the tub, each boy would say, 'Oh! I'm sorry, I didn't know anybody was in here!' Eieth caught on to the joke just about the time I opened the door, and it was I who got hit with a brand new bar of soap.

"I remember once," Alger recalled, "when one of George's pranks really got me into trouble with my father. It happened on the Fourth of July. My father believed in celebrating the occasion with plenty of fireworks and dozens of Roman candles. He was a proud man who ruled his family with a stern hand, and we respected his authority. He was the manager of seven departments in a large mens' furnishing store in town and, consequently, was an immaculate dresser. He owned drawers full of shirts, and he preferred them heavily starched. It was one of my jobs to see to it that my father's shirts were taken to the Chinese laundry that was located over near Morrison's Field. A few days before the holiday I took several of my father's shirts that were practically brand new over to the laundry.

"Well, I was walking across Morrison's Field early in the afternoon on the Fourth, and I bumped into George. Remembering my father's love for fireworks, he urged me to go back to the house and sneak some out, and we'd have some fun. I brought back a pocketful of firecrackers and several Roman candles. At about this time George noticed the back window of the Chinese laundry was open, and, devil that he was, he aimed the candles toward the open window. At least two went sailing through it. Well, the back room was used for drying the laundry, and as you may guess, the burning candles struck my father's shirts and burned large holes in two of them. It was an incredible coincidence, and one that I paid for several days later when the shirts came back and my father learned from the Chinaman what had happened. I got a good thrashing for it, but my father never said a word to George."

There were times, however, when George's deviltry was subordinated to an innate need to be a Good Samaritan. This side of George emerged in an incident that occurred at the Calumet YMCA when George was about twelve. A group of young kids was engaged in a little horseplay near the indoor pool. One of the older boys grabbed the hat from atop the head of a small boy and threw it across the pool. The hat landed on a ledge that fronted a window. George came into the swim room and found the small boy in tears. It was a bitter cold night, and George was dressed in his long corduroy coat and corduroy trousers tucked inside black, buckled arctics. His head was covered by a leather ear-lapper cap of the type used by aviators, and his hands were sealed inside large leather mittens. Without bothering to remove any of his clothing, George leaped up and caught hold of a steel pipe that ran over the pool; moving hand over hand he was able to make his way across it, and hanging monkey-style with one hand grasping the bar, he scooped up the hat, maneuvered himself around, and started back in the same tedious manner. Halfway across, perspiration caused one of his hands to slip from its mitten. Before he could get his exposed hand up to the pipe, out slipped the other one, and he went splashing into the water below. George removed his wet clothes and hung them over a radiator to dry. A friend who stayed with Gipp that night recalls they didn't get home until midnight.

Despite that untoward incident, some of young Gipp's happiest hours were spent at the Calumet YMCA. There he learned to swim and to play basketball, and there, in one of the second-floor game rooms, he got his introduction to the exacting art of pool shooting. George proved from the outset to be superior to his peers in every type of indoor competition that the "Y" had to offer; but it was the skill he demonstrated on Morrison's Field, the vacant lot behind his house, that set George apart from all of his competition. By the time he was eleven he showed so much talent with a bat and glove that Abner Doubleday might well have been overcome with joy. Boys his own age offered little in the way of competition for him, forcing him in the direction of much older boys. Lyman Frimodig, who was George's first and possibly only idol when the former starred in three sports at Calumet High School, said of Gipp, "He always wanted to play with the older boys. And they resented him, partly due to jealousy, I suspect, because of his superior talent. I used to feel sorry for him, and soon after we'd start to choose up sides, I'd pick George. But let me tell you, he was damn good. He just bubbled with enthusiasm. He'd chase foul balls all day long if you let him and never complain. He just wanted to play, and he was willing to do anything. You just had to see him for a minute with either a bat or glove to know he was a natural."

In 1908, during the annual Laurium foot race held on the Fourth of July, George distinguished himself by winning in a veritable breeze. In fact he got so far ahead of the field that near the finish line, in a mocking gesture unusual on his part, he stopped and waited until several of the racers came dangerously close before putting on a quick burst of speed that carried him across the finish line.

But George's first real local recognition lay just around the corner, when in 1910 he entered Calumet High School and went out for basketball the first winter.

3.

The Making of a Superstar

GEORGE Gipp was a surprise starter on the Calumet High School basketball team in the bone-chilling winter of 1910-11. In pre-season workouts George's repeated displays of uncanny speed and sharp-shooting combined with ball-handling wizardry gave him the nod over senior Walter Etu for one of the starting forward positions.

With Gipp in a line-up led by Lyman Frimodig, a flashy senior forward and candidate for All-State honors, the Calumet quintet peeled off twenty-four consecutive victories, which included, thanks to a mid-court set shot by Gipp with only eight seconds remaining, a one-point upset victory over mighty Marquette Normal. Also numbered among their victims was Calumet High's archrival, the local YMCA, which went down to two straight defeats at the hands of Gipp, Frimodig, and company, the last a 33-31 squeaker played before some seven hundred screaming fans at the "Y" gymnasium.

28

With their second victory over the local "Y," Coach Berg-man's quintet was crowned regional champs for the second straight season, thus earning the right to compete for the interregional championship against Negaunee High School at Negaunee. In a contest that saw the lead change twenty times, Negaunee, still smarting from a 60-21 pasting at the hands of Calumet the year before, went on to post a 37-32 up-set victory, thus bringing to an end one of the longest win-ning streaks in the state's history. Nevertheless, reporter Len Rautiola, covering the game for the *Keweenaw Miner*, had the following comment next day: "Calumet has one of the fastest and cleverest teams ever seen up this way. Gipp and Frimodig are excellent point-makers, and it's an indescrib-able joy to see just how well Gipp and Curto play together, pulling off some really fine combinations."

The contest against Negaunee High School is noteworthy since it marked the close of George's athletic career in high school.

Through the years any number of spurious stories have circulated about George's sports career at Calumet High. Newspapermen on the alert for good copy have used these stories freely without bothering to check the facts or the reliability of their sources. Consequently, much that has been written about George's early athletic career is nothing more than elaborate fables having as a common denominator some of the best examples of hyperbole to be found anywhere. One story, for example, claims that when playing hockey George was good for a goal just about every time he slapped a puck in the direction of the net. Another story relates that in a crucial basketball game George dumped in fifty-two points to emerge the game's hero. Regarding the former tale, we have it on the word of Paul Hogan, a sandlot baseball team-mate of Gipp's and one of the best amateur hockey players this country has ever produced, that George never learned how to skate. Concerning the latter story, there is no record anywhere to support its claim. Furthermore, it need only be pointed out that in George's time the rules called for a jump ball after the successful completion of each field goal, a rule that not only held down an individual's scoring but also eliminated the use of the fast break.

Although the accounts of Gipp's diamond feats would have been enough to bring a blush to the cheeks of Rogers Hornsby, the truth is that George never went out for baseball in high school. The same can be said for football, with one slight exception. Frederic Larson, a first-string center at Calumet High for three seasons, recalls George's having tried out for the team one fall, at which time he attended exactly one practice drill. Later on he made an occasional appearance at an afternoon scrimmage, limiting his activities to an hour or so of punting practice, purely for the fun of it. However, we do know that George sometimes played football in and around his home area in pre-Notre Dame days. We have it on the authority of Heartly Anderson, who played on several local amateur teams with Gipp during this time.

Finally, we have it on the incontrovertible testimony of several classmates of Gipp's that after his first year of high school he was unable to participate in sports because of an unwillingness to bring his grades up to the average required of a student athlete. That his grades were below average is not surprising since George, aside from disliking school, seems to have detested those subjects that required the memorization of countless pages of dull facts and figures. With school projects that encouraged creativity, it was a different matter entirely, as revealed by a poem written by him for a freshman English class. The verse reflects George's profound love of freedom, as well as a knack for humorous expression in a somewhat sardonic vein:

Now there is always a chance for poets to write
Of things that we see and that startle the sight,
Of how Beasley went around in his aeroplane true
With his head toward the green and his feet to the blue.
Now a picture of this how well I could paint,
If I were a Keats, but you see now I ain't.

Now if I were Shelley who also wrote poems
I'd tell of the paths thru the air that he wound,
I'd tell how he soared like a bird on high
While the crowd watched below with a prayer and a
     sigh.
I'd tell how he saw all the angels and saints
If I were a Keats, but of course now I ain't.

Now Gibbon they say wrote a history true
Of things that had happened afore me and you,
Of battles and wars and of wayward sons
Whose only ambition was great battles won,
Of great men I'd tell with their ways so quaint
If I were a Keats and I'm sorry I ain't.*

In his senior year his pranks rather than his grades accounted for most of George's tribulations. The chief task of
Calumet principal E. J. Hall, aside from the administrative
duties of his office, seems to have been the once-a-month expulsion of George Gipp from school. One expulsion resulted
from a prank George played with several statues situated on
the school grounds. Several buddies joined George in a search
of their family closets for odd pieces of clothing such as hats,
sox, ties, gloves, and scarves. The clothes went to dress up

---

*George's penmanship in the original copy was extraordinarily poor,
which prompted his teacher to make this annotation alongside a grade
of B: "Since you've acknowledged you're not a poet, don't assume the
penmanship of one for you haven't the poetic license to be illegible."

some of the more prominent examples of campus statuary. After learning the names of the culprits, Principal Hall gave a stern lecture on the principles of proper student behavior to George's accomplices and immediately suspended George for a period of two weeks. George's last suspension, however, occurring some weeks before graduation, came not because of a prank but rather because George had been caught along with a buddy smoking in the school hallway.

Meanwhile, George found a ready outlet for his enthusiasm for athletics at the YMCA. In his sophomore year he played forward for the basketball team sponsored by the Keckonen Hardware Store. The other forward post was held by George's friend and former teammate, Lyman Frimodig. Although not nearly as successful as they had been on the high-school team, the two sharp-shooters led the Keckonen five to a respectable first division finish. A year later, in 1913, the pair joined an excellent Calumet "Y" team that journeyed down to Ishpeming, Michigan to participate in a unique two-divisional tournament.

Held at the local "Y," the tournament featured both a high school and an independent division. On February 14 Calumet opened the independent class of the tournament against the Negaunee "Y," handing the badly outclassed Owls a humiliating 52-3 defeat in a contest that brought loud whoops and jeers from an amused crowd each time the Owls got possession of the ball and a standing ovation when they sank their only field goal late in the third quarter.

Coming back that same Friday night with only two hours' rest, Calumet, led by a brilliant, indefatigable Gipp, who pumped in twelve points and enthralled the throng with his bullet passes and snappy ball handling, drubbed the Ishpeming "Y" 30-18. Twenty-four hours later Calumet was on the floor again, this time against the Knights of King Arthur, in the divisional title match. Again it was Gipp, along with a hot-shooting Lyman Frimodig, who made the difference. Calumet rode to a surprisingly easy 44-15 triumph. But the night was far from over for Gipp and company. A large, sometimes happy, sometimes disgruntled crowd suddenly rose to its feet and refused to leave the gymnasium until the champs of both divisions were pitted against one another. Frightened tournament officials consented to this unreasonable demand, and for the fourth time in two evenings the boys from Calumet found themselves out in mid-court, awaiting the game-opening jump ball. This time their opponent was to be Ishpeming High School. The gruelling pace to which they had been subjected apparently had little effect on this fine Calumet team. They breezed by the high school champs 33-12, leaving no doubt in the minds of the departing fans which of the two divisional champs was the better one.

In after-game ceremonies the Calumet team was awarded the customary Gold Cup. For their individual performances each player was the recipient of a small gold medal. George finished the tournament with a thirty-three point total, good enough to place second in total individual points. Probably the best reward came to George and teammates alike the next morning when a local Ishpeming sports scribe wrote the following tribute to them: "The Calumet team, led by George Gipp and Lyman Frimodig, is the best team in the Upper Peninsula and maybe the best team in the state."

In 1914 a zealot named Gavrilo Princip assassinated the Archduke Ferdinand and thus precipitated World War I. In Hollywood that same year Pearl White starred in twenty bi-weekly installments of a serial that thrilled the movie-goers who rushed to see her in *The Perils of Pauline*. The year also marked George Gipp's graduation from Calumet High School, this unheralded event occurring some four months after he reached the age of nineteen.

Unlike most of his fellow classmates, George had not enrolled in such popular high school courses as carpentry, drawing, and blacksmithing. These courses, given under the aegis of the C&H Mining Company and taught in all of the high schools in the area, were considered a necessary part of a school's curriculum since nearly all of the graduates went from classroom to mining company without so much as a thought to the possibility of seeking other employment. With George it was different. According to close friends, the mere thought of being swallowed up by that giant corporation was repugnant to him. Consequently, he never saw fit to prepare himself for such an eventuality. Instead, he went to work for the Roehm Construction Company immediately upon graduation.

Whether George's decision was based on some remarkable foresight is immaterial, but it did prove shortly thereafter to have been a wise move. For in 1914 a union struggle threw copper mining in the Keweenaw into the throes of its first great crisis, one that was to persist for the next several years. In the end the triumph of unionism brought an unexpected end to copper mining in the Keweenaw, eventually forcing the migration of thousands of unemployed miners to Detroit, where a seeming madman by the name of Henry Ford was prepared to guarantee, in spite of the Depression, an unheard-of $5.00 a day, at the same time reducing the workday shift from nine to eight hours.

George escaped the miners' problems by avoiding employment at C&H. Instead, he worked at Roehm Construction for brief periods for about seven years, including parts of all his summer vacations away from Notre Dame. He could never have been considered a steady employee, even after joining the company full-time upon graduation from Calumet. Often in those years he suddenly would quit without apparent motivation, returning several months later without a suitable explanation for such unreasonable behavior. His most notable contribution to the company came the summer a dump truck he drove carried most of the crushed rock used in laying the first concrete road between Laurium and Ahmeek.

During his self-imposed layoffs from Roehm, George worked occasionally as a taxi driver in his hometown. His brief stint in this line of work was limited to the role of chauffeur for people who rented an automobile owned by the Richetta brothers of Laurium. The Richettas were local funeral directors and the first of their profession to substitute automobiles for horse-drawn carriages. Proprietors of a fashionable livery stable in town, the Richettas rented out horse-drawn rigs replete with buffalo-skin blankets for their occupants, and, as a sideline, the brothers maintained an automobile that was rented out to customers for all occasions. One of the last cars George drove for the Richettas was a Mitchell—a gigantic two-door sedan, jet black with a matching cloth top.

George got his first real opportunity to play baseball in the summer of 1915 when, as a center fielder, he joined a fine Laurium team, then a member of the highly touted Trolley League, one of the finest amateur baseball leagues in all of Michigan. George's first season turned out to be a great one. He hit for both average and distance, while bunting and running the bases with the authority and recklessness of a Ty Cobb. He roamed the outfield with the grace and speed of a young gazelle, gobbling up everything hit within a mile of him. Time and again his rifle arm threw out an overconfident base runner trying to gain an extra base. In short, George was as hot as that unusually torrid summer of '15 in the Upper Peninsula.

A week after the close of the regular season, Laurium was matched against Gay, the recent winner of the rival county league. Coming to bat in the last of the eighth and trailing by a run, the first two Laurium batters struck out swinging. The next batter up caught hold of a hanging curve ball and looped a single to right. Up stepped Gipp. With the cheers of several hundred fans echoing above the bleachers at the Laurium Driving Park, George ripped into a fast ball and sent it sailing beyond the confines of the ballpark. Joe Savinni, who followed Gipp in the batting order, recalls the homer: "There was a coal pile well beyond the center field area, and that ball was still soaring as it went over it. It was the longest drive ever hit by anybody up here."

In 1916 there were no organized amateur leagues in the Upper Peninsula. Most of the towns that were represented in the old Trolley League again fielded nines, but the games were played on a week-to-week basis. Not nearly as much baseball was played as in the previous year, but by midsummer George's spectacular playing with the Laurium nine had thrust him into the local spotlight. Some of the largest baseball crowds in the history of the area were turning up at local parks just to get a look at Laurium's great center fielder in action. And seldom, if ever, were they disappointed.

Old-time area ballplayers, some of whom went on to professional careers in the sport, still claim Gipp was the best they ever played with, probably the best they had ever seen. Most agree that George came closest in ability and appearance to the old Yankee Clipper, Joe DiMaggio. Like DiMag, who was still being conveyed via stroller at the time Gipp was giving opposing pitchers migraines, George employed a wide-open stance. He stood well back in the box, feet planted firmly, his bat resting on his right shoulder, gripped, in the manner of all power hitters, right down at the bottom. Unlike DiMag, however, a favorite idiosyncrasy of George's was to spit on the bat every time he stepped up to the plate.

Despite his growing fame, George's personal life had become a bog, stirred somewhat by a steady stream of promiscuous contacts. During this uncertain period he seems to have had no particular plan or purpose for his life. Most of his friends were card players, pool hustlers, or just plain pool-hall loafers, and for good reason—George was spending most of his time playing cards or shooting pool. One of his favorite haunts was Jimmy O'Brien's Pool Room, located about three blocks from George's home on Heckla Street. Occasionally, when George got bored with the local action, he'd hop a trolley and ride over to Calumet. His favorite place there was the Michigan Cafe, an ordinary saloon that had about four booths situated off to one side of the bar. It was here, or so some claim, that he learned everything there was to know about playing poker properly; his talent soon would be corroborated once he hit South Bend.

One old-timer recalls George during those days: "He wasn't exactly cocky, but he had no reverence for anybody or anything. He was winning a hell of a lot of money what with poker and pool, but he was throwing it away just as fast as it came to him. He just didn't seem to give a damn about anything."

With a large number of the more staid townspeople, the criticism of George was a bit more abrasive. They looked upon him as a lazy, worthless young man, destined to run out his life as a ne'er-do-well. And George made little effort to affect a more favorable image. For instance, in an area known to take its religion seriously, he was obstinate in his refusal to attend Sunday church services, even after his father had been appointed deacon of his church.

But unknown to everybody, George included, the whimsical hand of fate already had poked its finger into the affairs of young Mr. Gipp. It all began in 1909, when Indiana State Senator Robert Emmett Proctor formed a baseball team made up entirely of Notre Dame students and led them on a barnstorming tour of Michigan's Upper Peninsula. The senator, a *summa cum laude* graduate of Notre Dame's law school, had been a prominent attorney in Elkhart, Indiana since the turn of the century and had gained state-wide recognition as an avid sportsman, prone to sizable personal investments to encourage sports programs. His invasion of the Upper Peninsula met with less than spectacular results, the Notre Dame nine dropping every game they played in the first weeks of the tour. Morale had reached its nadir when Proctor decided it was time to dicker for the services of two well-known stars of the area. The negotiations were successful, and Paul Hogan and Wilbur Gray became temporary members of this once-exclusive Notre Dame nine.

Paul Hogan was a handsome young man, lean and muscular and with the suppleness of a panther. Like a handful of athletes of the era, he was an outstanding performer in more than one sport, excelling in baseball, football, track, and ice hockey. In baseball he was good enough to be offered a contract by the Boston Red Sox, which he declined to accept for what he said were personal reasons. As a hockey player Hogan was acclaimed by leading sportswriters as one of the best defensive players in America.

Wilbur T. "Dolly" Gray was an outstanding catcher, possessed of a fine throwing arm. A line-drive hitter, he usually got more than his fair share of safe hits. His not-too-secret ambition was to become the catcher for the Chicago White Sox. It was a tall order since it meant supplanting the formidable Ray Schalk, but then anybody who knew the cocky Gray could have told you that one thing the boy didn't lack was self-confidence.

With the addition of Hogan and Gray, the Notre Dame nine went on to win the rest of their scheduled games, turning a fiasco into a highly successful junket. Impressed by both his new-found stars, Senator Proctor made an offer to secure scholarships for them at his alma mater. Hogan declined almost immediately. Gray, on the other hand, was eager to accept the enticing offer but feared telling his father about it. After all, Notre Dame was a notorious Roman Catholic institution, and the Grays were themselves staunch Baptists of the equally notorious Midwestern variety. Surprisingly, the elder Gray consented in what appears to have been a triumph of common sense over prejudice. "Go anywhere if they'll give you a free education," was the elder Gray's reply.

Dolly went on to Notre Dame, where he starred on the baseball team for four years until his graduation in the spring of 1914. Many Notre Dame alumni remember the fiery Gray as having been one of the best players ever to strap on the tools of ignorance.

After graduation Gray joined a fine semi-pro team in Elkhart, Indiana. The team was owned by the seemingly omnipresent Proctor. Returning home from Elkhart in the late summer of 1916, Dolly chanced to meet George Gipp on a downtown Laurium street. At this time Gray proposed that George come down to South Bend. With George's baseball talent, Dolly was certain he could arrange an athletic scholarship for him. George was hesitant.

"I'm too old to try school again," George said. "Besides, I don't have any money."

Paul Hogan, who already had spoken to Gray about a scholarship for George, entered into the discussion several days later, and between the two they convinced George to give it a try. Dolly immediately contacted friends at the school, while George's older brother, Alexander, went around to a local butcher shop and borrowed enough money for his brother's train fare.

It is unlikely that Hogan, Gray, Alexander, or George himself had the least inkling of what lay ahead, when on that Indian summer day in early September 1916, George Gipp boarded a train at Calumet en route to the garish city of South Bend.

4.

Gipp Enters Notre Dame

GEORGE Gipp got his first look at South Bend from a seat aboard the old Hill Street trolley as it rumbled along to the south entrance of the Notre Dame campus. For George, away from home for the first time in his life, the ride must have seemed as eerie and desolate as a trolley trip to Mars. For one thing, he did not have the slightest notion of what to expect once he got to Notre Dame; even worse, he didn't know what was going to be expected of him. George was coming there with no idea as to what his academic pursuits would be. What's more, he was arriving in town with very little money in his pocket.

According to a neighbor, George left Laurium with scarcely more than the clothes on his back. Gipp, reflecting on his first days at Notre Dame, told a friend back home, "I was really upset when I got to Notre Dame, mainly on account of I didn't have much money. But they were pretty good about it. And after awhile, everything was jake."

A student burdened with financial troubles might have found himself caught in one embarrassing situation after another had he chosen to matriculate at the University of Michigan or any of the other larger, more prestigious Midwestern schools. Luckily for George, however, this was not likely to happen in South Bend. At Notre Dame students with little or no money in their pockets were commonplace. The main reason for this was simple—Notre Dame was basically a poor boys' college, a fact that was not always apparent to the naked eye.

Scenically, the school created an illusion of great wealth and beauty, what with its seemingly endless expanse of virgin greenery that supported, at ideally situated intervals, a number of large, sturdy, brick edifices that lent themselves favorably to an atmosphere of quiet, subdued richness. Situated on the placid shores of St. Mary's Lake, the school was a splendid example of Old World architecture, poignantly typified by a weather-worn, yellow-brick edifice that serves to this day as its main building, on top of which is mounted the famous Golden Dome of Our Lady, a breathtakingly beautiful sight set against an azure Midwestern sky. From her queenly perch she stands arms outstretched, as though to summon all who gaze upon her to come forth and feel the warmth of her motherly compassion. The loftiness of her intent seems to touch the tree-shaded lanes that lace the quadrangle below. The less imposing bronze statue of the school's first president, Father Edward Sorin, stands like a sentinel on the south side of the campus, and off at a distance the majestic spire of the Sacred Heart Church points toward the heavens.

In George Gipp's day the number of young men able to draw inspiration from this beatific atmosphere was surprisingly few. At the time of his matriculation there were scarcely nine hundred full-time students enrolled at Notre Dame, nearly all of whom were in residence at the half-dozen dormitories scattered about the campus: Brownson, Washington, Badin, Sorin, Holy Cross, and Corby. Another dormitory, Walsh, referred to as the "millionaires' hall," was reserved exclusively for the more affluent students. The school itself, not nearly as pretentious as Walsh Hall, was composed of the colleges of Arts and Letters, Science, Law, and Engineering.

Although its list of colleges was hardly striking by comparison with that of many other Midwestern institutions, the progress of Notre Dame in the course of seventy-five years was remarkable, especially in view of an early history marred by adversity that easily could have caused the school's downfall had it not been for the courage and tenacity displayed by those responsible for Notre Dame's survival. It is an interesting history and one that should be touched upon briefly if only to support a long-held contention of many sports fans that Notre Dame is invincible. Its invincibility, as we shall see, transcends mere athletics.

Begun as a Catholic mission in 1830, Notre Dame is situated on a large tract of land in northern Indiana, an area of the Midwest that was once the property of Chief Leopold Pokagon and the Potawatomi tribe. The mission, built by Father Stephen T. Badin, was erected to serve the spiritual needs of the chief's people, who more than a half-century before had been converted by a Jesuit priest, Claude Allouez.

The mission flourished under the ambitious Badin; in less than a year a school and orphanage were established, and the parish itself expanded to encompass a radius of fifty miles. Unfortunately, this tiny outpost of Christianity soon found itself caught up in the wake of the white man's western migration, a migration that would eventually signal the mission's end. In 1838 the mission was forced to close its doors shortly after a contingent of US troops moved into the wilderness area to enforce a government decree that evicted the Potawatomis from their homeland forever.

Father Badin's mission with its nine hundred acres of virgin forest remained abandoned for four years. Then on November 16, 1842, Father Edward Sorin and seven brothers belonging to the Congregation of the Holy Cross loaded an ox cart at their mission near Vincennes and set out in search of this remote outpost, which they hoped would provide the proper setting on which to build a great Catholic university. It was an arduous journey, marked by heavy snows and blinding, blistering winds that signaled the start of the coldest winter on record in North America since 1607. The trip lasted eleven days and was conducted with the aid of the nephew of a local fur trader, Alexis Coquillard.* When Father Sorin and his weary fellow-travelers reached the abandoned mission, they knelt down in the snow and thankfully consecrated the land to the Blessed Virgin Mary, a gesture many Roman Catholics will tell you was greatly responsible for the many boons the school has enjoyed through the years.

Father Sorin's group cleared away a large swath of forest, the timber of which was used to construct a larger chapel. With the aid of neighboring settlers, they scooped clay from marl beds along the shores of nearby St. Mary's Lake, molded it into brick, and baked it in the community kiln. The finished product was then used to construct the first college building.

By 1844 Father Sorin was able to add a novitiate. More important, with the construction of only one college building to his credit, he was able to wangle a charter from the State of Indiana to establish a college. With this grant Notre Dame University came into being.

---

*The teenage Coquillard was soon to earn the distinction of becoming Notre Dame's first scholar.

In the beginning the school did not offer student scholarships. Rather, the policy of the founding fathers was to find poor boys desirous of learning a trade and to educate them in a fashion that would enable them to succeed in the ordinary walks of life. Despite this noble purpose, the problems that faced the new school from the outset were enormous. The major problem, as might be expected, was a constant need for finances to support existing programs. In addition to this woe, the school was struck by several severe outbreaks of cholera and malaria and a succession of disastrous fires. One such conflagration, which occurred in 1879, destroyed several major buildings and brought the institution to the brink of extinction. But thanks to a succession of faithful custodians, Notre Dame was able to survive, and what's more, to prosper. Perhaps the finest tribute paid these men is to be found in the 1920 edition of *The Dome*, the school's yearbook: "Our school was built by the dreams and toil of her own, and never once did we seek endowment."

Even without endowment Notre Dame found itself in a position to provide a free education for large numbers of young men who otherwise might never have been able to attend an institution of higher learning. Long after it had taken on an air of subtle sophistication and had begun to offer a bachelor's degree, the school still lent a sympathetic hand to needy young men desirous of obtaining further formal education. This worthwhile enterprise was accomplished by the granting of both academic and athletic scholarships.

Furthermore, the school offered a job plan that was designed to help students meet their everyday expenses. Often Notre Dame itself was able to provide suitable employment. When no openings were to be found at the school, every effort was made by administrators to secure suitable outside employment for a student.

One of the best-known beneficiaries of this plan was George

Gipp, who, upon enrollment, was put to work waiting on tables at Brownson Hall. Situated directly beneath the Golden Dome, Brownson was the hall to which all freshmen were assigned and held the only student dining room on campus. Because he was assigned the station nearest the kitchen, George was required to work two tables instead of the customary one. Students who remember him as a waiter during his first semester at Notre Dame say that he was a good one, always polite and courteous, whose tables were promptly served and cleared. Others recall that he cut a handsome figure in the stiffly starched white jacket he wore.

By taking the job as waiter, George became the second Notre Dame student destined to achieve national fame to take advantage of the job plan in less than a decade. The other was the indefatigable Knute Rockne, who, as a freshman in 1910, used the plan to its fullest advantage by holding down six different jobs at the same time, a feat which has never been equalled by a student at South Bend.

Despite its maintenance of a job plan, rumors still persisted on the Notre Dame campus in Gipp's day that certain star athletes had been the recipients of generous gratuities; the money, let it be said, was rumored to come not from the school itself but rather from some of the more successful alumni who managed to maintain more than a passing interest in their alma mater's sports program. Supposedly, the favorite method used by these benefactors to reward a star performer was the surreptitious transfer of a sealed envelope at some convenient time and place. As much as $200 was said to have been involved in some of these transactions, depending largely on the status of the athlete involved. Another method sometimes used was to grant an athlete unconditional use of a benefactor's charge account at an exclusive South Bend men's store. Despite the persistence of such rumors, none of the charges were ever proved. What is more important here is that although George enjoyed top status among the school's stars, never once was his name linked to such questionable transactions. His best friend, Hunk Anderson, himself free from such rumors, says the reason for this was simple: "George made his own way. What he got he got on his own, and everybody knew it." This quality of independence displayed so often by Gipp was to have a lasting impression on the equally independent Anderson.

One is struck by the large number of the school's early diamond stars whose names were linked to those members of the alumni known for their generosity. However, it takes only a glance at the history of Notre Dame to understand why this is so. Up until Knute Rockne and George Gipp combined to make *Notre Dame* synonymous with *football*, baseball enjoyed an overwhelming edge in popularity at South Bend. And its history as it relates to the school is every bit as interesting as the sport that was to supplant it in campus prestige.

As early as 1869 baseball was being played on the campus of Notre Dame. That the sport was limited to intramural competition in no way hindered the chances of an ambitious young man with a potential for diamond stardom from obtaining an athletic scholarship from the school. In fact, shortly after the Civil War, a young man who was to become one of the greatest baseball players of all time gained entrance into Notre Dame in this manner. His name was Adrian Constantine "Cap" Anson. In a career that spanned twenty-six seasons—five more than the immortal Babe—Anson, as a member of the Chicago Cubs, led the National League in hitting for two consecutive seasons: 1887 and 1888. His greatest achievements came shortly before, however, when as a player-manager he led his teams to five National League pennants.

Cap Anson may have been the first Notre Damer to make

it to the top, but he was by no means the last. Following in his footsteps were such accomplished big-leaguers as Roger Bresnahan, Bert Daniels, Long Cy Williams, George Cutshaw, and Red Murray. By 1920 the school was able to boast of having sent twenty men to the major leagues. What makes this number all the more impressive is that the school did not begin to participate in intercollegiate baseball until 1892.

During this span of twenty-eight years, the best teams to represent the school were those that played from 1906 through 1908, compiling a total of sixty wins against only nine losses. The 1908 squad, which won twenty of its games while dropping only one, became the first to represent the school beyond the confines of the Middle West, traveling all the way to the East Coast, where it defeated both Dartmouth and Vermont. Several years later Notre Dame teams played host to Arkansas, West Virginia, and Penn State. In 1913 the South Benders went on a barnstorming tour of the East, playing Pennsylvania, Navy, Fordham, Army, and Catholic University. The contest with Army—won by the Cadets 3-0—marked the first sports competition between the two schools. More significantly, it set the stage for the football rivalry that was soon to follow. William Cutter, then the Notre Dame graduate manager, remembers that head football coach Jesse Harper, taking his cue from the baseball team, sat down and wrote letters to many athletic directors in hopes of arranging gridiron games between Notre Dame and some of the more powerful schools from other sections of the country. One of the schools Harper wrote to was Army. Shortly thereafter he received a favorable reply to his inquiry. Cutter arranged for and later signed the contract for the first football game between Army and Notre Dame.

Although the school's founding father, Edward Sorin, had a reputation as an expert marble shooter not in the least adverse to competing against the more proficient of his elementary-grade students,* it is highly unlikely that he ever imagined that the national recognition he sought for his school would come not from its academic rating but rather from a knack for turning out some of the finest football teams ever produced by any college in the country. Fortunately for Notre Dame, those who followed in Father Sorin's footsteps not only were willing to accept this manner of achieving recognition but bent every effort to perpetuate a winning football tradition. As time has shown, it was well worth their efforts. Football not only brought Notre Dame national recognition, but it also helped pay the bills. Football also provided the school's most famous coach, Knute Rockne, with a favorite story, which concerned a man who visited Notre Dame and found that everybody, including the president, carried a football and was ready at a moment's notice to hip into the backfield shift. "The funny part of that story," Rockne would conclude, "is that everybody believes it."

Much of the credit for the creation of such an atmosphere belongs to a former president of the university, Father John W. Cavanaugh. During his tenure of office, Father Cavanaugh was concerned primarily with the building of an extensive intramural sports program. He was convinced that athletics was both physically and mentally beneficial, and he wanted to be certain that all of his students had easy access to those benefits. It was not his intention, however, to encourage intercollegiate competition for the simple reason that in the past varsity sports always had lost money for the school. To implement his program, the wily priest enticed football coach Jesse Harper away from his post at nearby Wabash College and brought him to Notre Dame. Father Cavanaugh rewarded Harper for his switch by appointing him both athletic director and head coach of football.

---

*From its inception Notre Dame was one of the few colleges in America that had both elementary and high-school facilities.

A proven organizer, Harper first arranged an extensive interhall, interclass competitive plan; only after this was accomplished was he granted permission to try to schedule some varsity sports contests with schools from other sections of the country. Harper, to no one's surprise, least of all Father Cavanaugh's, was spectacularly successful in his efforts. He set up one of the school's first intramural sports programs, one that was to become the envy of every other college in the Midwest. He also managed to allot himself as much time as was needed to lift Notre Dame football up out of its doldrums and start it on the long road that would lead to national recognition.

When George Gipp got to Notre Dame there were between thirty-five and forty campus teams engaged in this energetic intramural sports program. In front of every hall there was a small campus where students kicked footballs back and forth in their free hours. Since every able-bodied student was expected to join his hall's team, George obliged. Three days after he took up residence at Brownson Hall he signed up with its football team. It turned out to be an ephemeral commitment. After the first practice session, George quit the team abruptly without giving anybody a satisfactory explanation for this hasty decision.

The main reason for Gipp's action might have been that he was going through a difficult transitional period, made all the more difficult by his age and temperament. We know from his days at Calumet High School that student life was never one of his great loves; yet he found himself, two years after graduation, thrust back into school. Nevertheless, he seems at this time to have been willing to give it another try. Like most of his freshman classmates he carried a full workload, having signed up for courses in English, history, biology, political science, and German. We have proof that George was able to maintain passing grades in all of these subjects. We have no such proof, however, that he was able to adjust psychologically to student life that first semester at Notre Dame.

Going on the recollections of friends and classmates, one is led to believe that George was going through a difficult period. For one thing, he was never able to overcome the distinction of being three years the senior of most of his classmates. Consequently, he often appeared to be restless, uncomfortable, and somewhat remote in their presence. Often, classmates who tried to befriend him at this time were prone to misinterpret his uneasy attitude as one of aloofness, and as a result George enjoyed little popularity. Except for the occasional exchange of amenities with another student, his rich baritone voice, which Rockne once described as "warm, vibrant, and full of life," seldom echoed either inside or outside the classroom. The sound of his voice remained almost as much a secret as the severe sore throats he suffered during this period, which were caused in part by chronically infected tonsils that had plagued him since childhood.

That Gipp was something of a misfit during his first months at South Bend can be seen from the observation of one young man who got to know George fairly well: "He didn't seem to care as much about clothes as did the rest of us. He was a modest dresser whose preference in clothes was usually corduroy slacks and a dress shirt open at the collar. What I remember most about his dress was his tweed cap and a shiny, weather-beaten leather jacket of the type that aviators used to wear. Regarding the man himself, let me just say this: he wasn't the easiest guy to get to know."

This observation of Gipp was partly corroborated by Rockne, who, reflecting on George's early days at school, said, "He stayed mostly to himself, lived quietly, and had few friends. He was pleasant without being cheerful, affable without being congenial. He appeared just too sure of himself."

Another young man who befriended George at this time

was Walter Miller, himself a distinguished Notre Dame football player. "I remember seeing him come into the recreation room quite often. He was always alone. He'd spend maybe an hour or two shooting pool all by himself. I used to enjoy watching him shoot pool as he really could handle a cue stick. As I remember, it was nothing for him to run off upwards of eighty balls without a miss. For all the times I saw him do this I don't recall his ever saying as much as two words to anybody."

Unfortunately, George never thought to leave behind anything that might give us an indication of his own feelings at this time of his life. He kept no diary, and he seldom talked about himself. He did deign to write letters, but his output was meager. What's more, only two letters written by him have been uncovered. One of them, found by Jim Beach many years ago and reported in his book, *A History of Notre Dame Football*, was written at this time of George's life and deserves to be put down here. Written to a friend back home, the letter offers us a rare glimpse of that side of Gipp he so painstakingly hid from the public, a side that was tinged with anxiety, remorse, and more than a little self-pity:

I got here alright and got away with a pretty good start. Not so much my fault as the school's . . . I'm in a mood tonight where I'd like to go straight up. I want to come and go when I please. Sometimes I wonder what I'm here for. For awhile I felt decidedly human. But I can't seem to shake this recurring grouch I've got. It isn't a grouch exactly but it's something that makes me feel that I'm all wrong and will stay that way. Don't think that I'm not trying hard to get rid of it. Tonight is the first time I've felt like this since I've been down here. I'd like to give up and quit right now, chuck everything and go anywhere . . . Now I know that I'm unlucky.

What is curious about this letter is that George, in a rare moment in which he attempts to pour out his heart, does not mention anything about religion. Ordinarily one would expect that someone reared in a home that espoused strict adherence to Protestantism might find it difficult adapting to Notre Dame's atmosphere of Roman Catholicism. Gipp, however, seems to have had no problem regarding the religious atmosphere at the school. This was more than could be said of his mother, who, from the outset, had been opposed to her son's entering Notre Dame. The reason for her objection was as simple as it was understandable: she saw the priests not as educators but as instruments of the Church they represented. Consequently, she feared that these tools of Roman Catholicism would succeed in converting her son. As we shall see, her fear was not totally without grounds.

Meanwhile, George was able to avoid religion with the determination, if not the clamor, of a confirmed atheist. Even so, religion provides us with the best example of George's wit during this uncertain time of his life. His room at Brownson was situated next to the shower room. After being chided by a roommate for being a heretic in a school of Orthodox lambs, George merely smiled, pointed to the shower room, and said, "*I'm* the holy one around here. Cleanliness is always next to Godliness."

Perhaps his humor saved him during this most trying time. Had he been unable to look at his situation or himself with a certain degree of humor, chances are he might have taken his own advice about giving up and going anywhere. Given the benefit of hindsight, we are aware of the tragic consequences such a decision would have had, not only for him but for Notre Dame as well. For we can see Knute Rockne lurking about the campus while Gipp moves unwittingly toward him; both of them men of destiny and as yet total strangers; neither one aware of the impact their eventual collision would produce.

5.

A Freshman Phenom

To the American sports fan the meeting at Ujiji between Henry Morton Stanley and Dr. David Livingstone pales by comparison to the legendary encounter of Knute Rockne and George Gipp some forty-six years later at a place called South Bend. The attempt to compare these two meetings might seem frivolous, but of one thing there can be no doubt whatsoever—down through the years each has enjoyed its full share of publicity. Regarding the latter, it has been written about in books, magazines, and newspapers; it has even been recreated with a commendable degree of accuracy in a Hollywood movie, not to mention the countless retellings it has enjoyed at football banquets, alumni gatherings, or just about every other occasion when lovers of sports congregate to idle away a few hours.

For the most part these accounts of the legendary meeting are basically correct, varying occasionally on some minor

53

detail. It is best, however, in striving for accuracy, to rely on the testimony of both principals. Gipp, unfortunately, did not leave behind his recollection of it. Luckily for us, however, Knute Rockne did. In an article written over a quarter of a century ago for *Collier's Weekly*, the Irish mentor put down a detailed account of the meeting:

> I first met George Gipp on a football field. It was and is a habit of mine to stroll to the practice field and observe groups of freshmen or nondescript students kicking footballs around. Once in a great while you can spot, among these clumsy beginners, genuine talent.
>
> On one early Autumn afternoon in 1916 the practice field was all but deserted. A tall lad in everyday campus clothes was booting a football to a boy in a playing suit who kicked it back. The uniformed lad was a candidate for the freshman team. Their play seemed nothing more than the usual duet of punts between a football aspirant and some hall friend or roommate who had come out to oblige. The style of the taller boy caught my eye. He picked up the ball, poised his body with natural grace, slid the ball to the ground, and drop kicked with perfect ease—fifty yards. For about ten minutes I watched him. His kicks were far and placed evidently where he wanted them to go to give the other player catching practice. Here, I thought, was somebody worth examining. When he strolled from the field as if bored, I stopped him.
>
> "What's your name?" I asked.
>
> Most freshmen regard the football coach as if he's a deity on duty for the season. This boy was almost indifferent. "Gipp," he said, "George Gipp. I come from Laurium, Michigan."
>
> "Played high school football?" I asked.
>
> "No," he said, "don't particularly care for football. Baseball's my game."
>
> "What led you to come to Notre Dame?" I asked.
>
> "Friends of mine are here," he said.
>
> "Put on a football suit tomorrow," I invited, "and come out with the freshmen scrubs. I think you'll make a football player."

The lad with Gipp stared pop-eyed.

"Why," he said, "he's kicking those punts and drops with ordinary low shoes. What'll he do with football boots?"

The question posed to Rockne by that anonymous young man was soon to be answered when on the very next day a reluctant George Gipp turned out for freshman football practice. The student charged with passing out athletic equipment that day, after tossing a pair of battered football shoes at George, said to him, "Here, these shoes were once worn by Ray Eichenlaub."*

Had the equipment manager bothered to come out later and observe the practice session, he would have seen that fate had chosen him that day to outfit the young man whose name was to displace that of Eichenlaub's on the lips of his successors in the equipment room at Notre Dame. For on the very first play of the scrub game, the very first time he carried the ball, Gipp galloped unmolested through a stunned freshman line for a touchdown. That was just the beginning. Knocking about with the freshman squad for about a month under the watchful eye of Rockne, George consistently displayed the qualities destined to make him a star of the first magnitude. Although still untried in competition, he ran, passed, and kicked with the poise and confidence of a veteran.

Standing alongside freshmen coach Fitzgerald one afternoon, Rockne was so impressed with what he saw that he decided to broach a plan involving Gipp to Jesse Harper, a plan designed to help the varsity defeat Army that season. The plan was as brilliant as it was simple, and it was the first revelation of the ingenuity Rockne was later to display so abundantly in his role as head coach. In preparation for the

---

*This was a stock remark designed solely for the purpose of humbling any scrub who might be weighted down a bit by a sense of self-importance. Eichenlaub, a Notre Dame star from 1910 through 1914, played fullback on the varsity team for four years.

Army game Rockne knew, as well as Harper, that if Notre Dame wished to beat the Cadets, they first had to stop Elmer Q. Oliphant. A job, as the saying goes, that was much easier said than done.

Oliphant was a superstar, without a doubt one of the best all-around athletes in the history of West Point. Before his transfer to the Academy, he had been a star performer in just about every sport offered at Purdue University, and when he got to West Point he took right up where he had left off at Lafayette. As a baseball player he was a veritable bull with a bat; many of his record clouts are said to have hit the road in front of Cullum Hall before bouncing against that venerable old building, a distance equal to that of the more memorable drives delivered by the immortal Babe. Despite this great ability as a diamond performer, Oliphant, like Gipp, had to rely in the end on football to achieve fame.

In this most grueling of contact sports, Oliphant had all of the qualities needed to reach the top. He possessed unusual speed and great strength, and once he got a pigskin tucked underneath his arm he just naturally made all the right moves, moves that were perfectly complemented by unbelievable poise and supreme self-confidence.

In a collegiate career that was in its twilight at the time of George Gipp's emergence, Oliphant had not only proved himself to be one of the best ball-toters of all time but had succeeded in gaining a reputation as one of the experts in the art of drop kicking. Perhaps the best compliment ever paid Oliphant came from an opponent who said of the great Army star: "Trying to stop a charging Oliphant was equivalent to standing in front of a speeding locomotive, and just about as foolhardy."

In the week that preceded the Army-Notre Dame game at West Point, Knute Rockne was certain that he had come up with the perfect method by which to derail the great Army back. In essence the plan called for drilling a talented scrub back until he was able to do a perfect imitation of Oliphant. The player Rockne recommended to Harper for this difficult task was none other than George Gipp. After watching George work out with the freshmen, Rockne was positive he could carry off the assignment. Rockne was just as certain that once the Irish defense became familiar with Oliphant's style of ball-carrying, they would have little trouble stopping Army once the game got under way.

Rockne later recalled that Gipp showed no emotion when approached with the idea. "All right," he said, "if you think I can do any good."

For the next three days Rockne personally took George in hand. He made him "vary his pace, break his runs, and cut back and dodge." Rockne recalled that George was extremely patient, even during the dull repetition in slow motion of every part of a long broken field run. Next George was initiated into the veering style of Oliphant's ball carrying. And though the varsity had been primed to stop Gipp, Rockne remembered that once George was given the ball he swept wide around end, sped past the secondary with apparent ease, and went the distance for a touchdown. A perfect imitation of Oliphant.

Unfortunately for Notre Dame, Rockne's ingenious plan proved to be a failure, for on November 4 the Cadets, led by an unstoppable Oliphant, walloped the Fighting Irish 30-10. Later the wily Rockne came up with a master alibi to explain the dismal failure of his master plan. Confronted by a reporter, Rockne said, "The only drawback was that in the actual game with Army, Oliphant gave a perfect imitation of Gipp."

The day before Oliphant sped by the Gold and Blue line like a locomotive past a ghost town, George Gipp saw his first real action. On Friday, November 3, the frosh opened its abbreviated season against St. Viator's, a junior college from which Bishop Fulton J. Sheen was an early graduate. This distinction, had it been noteworthy back then, would still have proved of no value to the school's freshman gridmen once the unstoppable Mr. Gipp swung into action. With the score tied at 7-7 early in the third quarter, Coach Fitzgerald inserted George into the line-up for the first time that afternoon; Gipp responded quickly by booting a successful drop kick that resulted in his team's 10-7 victory.

On November 11 the frosh journeyed to Kalamazoo, Michigan to play Western State Normal (now Western Michigan University). Led by their newly appointed team captain, George Gipp (a rare honor for a backfield man at Notre Dame), the Irish freshmen were able to hold their own for three quarters against the heavier, more aggressive Normalites who, like their opponents, had come into the game unbeaten.

Late in the fourth quarter, with the score knotted at 7-7 and the strain of a hard-fought contest beginning to tell on both sides, the South Benders found themselves faced with a fourth-down situation, the ball resting on their own 38-yard line and long yardage needed for a first down. Aware that the clock showed less than three minutes left to play and content to settle for a tie, quarterback Frank Thomas called for a punt.

George Gipp protested. "Why settle for a tie?" he pleaded. "Let me try a drop kick."

"Just punt," replied Thomas emphatically.

Notre Dame came out of the huddle and lined up slowly with George dropping back to receive the snap from center. What happened next is best described by Walter Olsen, who played the safety post for Western State Normal that day: "I had caught a couple of 50-yard punts of Gipp's during the game, so naturally I was plenty far back, figuring it was another punt as it was fourth down. The ball came through the air like a line drive in baseball and to my surprise went sailing over the crossbar for the 3 points that beat us 10-7."

Another Normalite who has bitter memories of that particular incident is Warren "Goose" Allen. Converted into a linesman after a brilliant career as a backfield man on his Dowagiac, Michigan high-school team, Allen had just come into the game as a substitute: "I was sent in at right tackle to try to block what we all expected was going to be a punt. I remember it was a low kick that went between the goal posts, which were situated right on the goal line in those days. This was our first loss in five years," Allen recalls, "and it really rocked our prestige. It was a hard loss to take."

On a happier note, there was at least one person in the stands that afternoon who must have gotten almost as big a thrill at witnessing the game-winning drop kick as George had had in executing it. His name was Matthew Gipp, George's older brother and the second of the immediate family living in Kalamazoo at the time. The other was Dorothy, the baby of the family. In an interview given to a local newspaper thirty years later, Dorothy, or Dolly as she preferred to be addressed, recalled that she gave a party at her home the evening following the game in honor of her brother George. In retrospect the least George deserved for his gridiron efforts that day was a party in his honor. Of the 216 total yards run up by the Notre Dame frosh against Western State Normal, George was personally responsible for 174. And while the party must have pleased him, the topper to his great performance came the next day when George made the nation's sports headlines by virtue of his drop kick, which had been entered into the record book as measuring 62 yards—a drop kick that remains to this day as the second longest in the history of collegiate football. Despite George's great proficiency in this department, the record kick proved to be the penultimate one in his career and the last of his freshman career. For when the frosh closed out their three-game schedule against Kalamazoo College's frosh, they were never in a position where a drop kick of George's might have proved worthwhile. From the outset the South Benders found themselves completely outclassed, going down to defeat by the humiliating score of 34-7. However, John Thomson and Forrest Strome, both of whom starred for Kalamazoo that day, remember that Notre Dame's only score came on a long touchdown run by Gipp.

Meanwhile, George had become an overnight sensation on campus. Despite this flash flood of adulation, he never once let himself be drowned by feelings of self-importance. From all accounts he behaved with the same quiet dignity that was the hallmark of the man himself. When advised that there was a sudden vacancy for a white-collar worker at the school, George gracefully declined the offer, stating that he preferred to remain a waiter for the rest of the semester. Nor was there any marked change in his relationship with fellow students; he remained courteous and considerate, but as remote as ever. There was no change in his relationship with his teammates, either. As one member of that freshman team put it, "George never let his play go to his head. I don't remember him once displaying even a hint of condescension in his relations with me, or with any other player for that matter."

Despite his reluctance to take advantage of the prestige that was now his, he was nevertheless still very much the main topic of conversation on campus when school let out for the Christmas holiday, at which time he returned home to spend the allotted two weeks with family and friends. The visit, it turns out, came frighteningly close to putting an abrupt end to George Gipp's college career.

Home less than a week, George soon fell back into the

familiar routine that had marked his pre-Notre Dame existence—playing poker and pool to sustain himself. Friends who
recall this period say that George was a big winner in both
pool and poker, but because of his inherent generosity he
lent away most of his winnings. As a result, when the time
came for him to return to Notre Dame, he did not have
enough money to purchase a train ticket. Despite his predica-
ment, George appeared to be in very good spirits, so it came
as no surprise to his friends when he announced quite suddenly that he had decided against returning to Notre Dame.
The reason he gave for his decision was lack of money. With
several of his closest friends, however, George was a bit more
candid, admitting that he no longer could tolerate the restric-
tive life of a student.

What George apparently had overlooked when he gave
lack of money as an excuse for not returning to Notre Dame
was that he had friends, friends who had no intention of
letting a little thing like train fare stand in the way of a
college education. What happened next is best described by
George's baseball teammate, Joe Savinni: "As soon as it was
learned George was short the money for a train ticket, all of
his friends got together and took up a collection for him.
When we got enough collected, we went over to the depot
in Calumet and bought his ticket. Later, when we made him
a present of it, I detected in his attitude that he was a bit disappointed. I suppose at the time he was quite disillusioned
with college life."

Back in school once again, George worked out with the
freshman basketball team that winter on Notre Dame's dirt-
floor gymnasium. He appeared briefly in one game at the
start of the season before quitting the team unexpectedly. He
also enjoyed a brief stint as a member of the track team during
this time, and in the spring he showed up one day at freshman baseball practice. It turns out he only played one game

with the team, however. In the late innings of this game he was called on by his manager, a senior in the undergraduate school, to bunt. Instead of following orders, he swung away and sent a tremendous home run into deep left field. Trotting back to the dugout after having circled the bases, he was confronted by an irate manager who demanded to know why he had disobeyed orders. "It's too hot today to run bases," was Gipp's reply. The next day he turned in his uniform.

On March 30 George was among a host of eager young hopefuls who, along with a handful of varsity holdovers, swarmed over Cartier Field at the opening of spring football practice. An interesting highlight of this otherwise routine six-week drill occurred on April 3, when an exhibition contest was staged between the freshman squad and a team composed of alumni. This game, a forerunner of the annual alumni-varsity skirmish at Notre Dame, featured Knute Rockne as the alumni quarterback, with Gipp his counterpart on the freshman squad. When the final whistle blew, the freshmen had come out on the short end, 14-7. The losers' only score came in the closing minutes of the fray and was the result of some fine pin-point passing by Gipp that spurred an 80-yard touchdown drive.

Although the game had no significance other than the interjection of a little fun into the drills, both Harper and Rockne came away from it thoroughly pleased, each one visualizing an unbeaten season come next fall. The prospect looked all the brighter after their first good look at that former freshman phenomenon, George Gipp.

6.

Gipp Makes the Varsity

On April 2, 1917, President Woodrow Wilson called for a declaration of war on Germany. With his call to arms Wilson made a dramatic appeal for support of his proposed action by stating, "The world must be made safe for democracy."

This appeal produced the desired effect on a general public that heretofore had been tepid about any military involvement in the war sweeping across Europe. Inside of a week hundreds of thousands of young men, overwhelmed with a sense of patriotism, rushed to their nearest recruiting stations to enlist. However, even after this rash of enlistments, there were less than a quarter of a million men in uniform. Consequently, a draft bill was pushed through Congress. The effectiveness of conscription was acutely illustrated when on January 5, between the hours of 7:00 A.M. and 7:00 P.M., nearly ten million men went to their local polling places to register for the draft.

When Gipp returned home to spend his summer vacation in '17 (on June 14, according to a brief news item appearing in the *Daily Mining Gazette*), many of his buddies of baseball days already had joined the Army. The Keweenaw baseball season had begun some weeks before, but it bore only a faint resemblance to those of bygone summers. For one thing there were no organized leagues in operation, and less than a half-dozen towns even bothered to field teams. Moreover, the caliber of ball played was shockingly bad. The season could have been judged a complete fiasco had it not been for one saving grace—all of the proceeds from games played that summer went to benefit worthy organizations, such as the American Red Cross, the YMCA, and the more provincial Michigan Engineers' Mess Fund.

Shortly after being rehired as a dump-truck driver for Roehm Construction, George joined the Laurium baseball team, a move that was to prove beneficial to both parties. For Laurium the addition of Gipp made it the most popular team in the area. For George the move reunited him with one of his favorite teammates, Ed Tobola.

Several days after signing up to play with his hometown nine, George made his first local appearance of the season on June 26 in a game against Albion-Wolverine, played at the Laurium Driving Park. About two thousand fans turned out for the game, the proceeds of which, totaling $500, went to the Calumet branch of the Red Cross. The victory, by a score of 9-5, went to Albion-Wolverine. This despite an auspicious debut by Gipp, who collected three hits and drove in an equal number of runs, all of which, incidentally, came off an erstwhile teammate, Pete Murphy, who started on the mound for Albion.

On July 1, in a game played at the Laurium Driving Park for the benefit of the Michigan Engineers' Mess Fund, Laurium absorbed its second setback with Gipp in the line-up. This time it was Gay, a powerhouse from the Iron Country, that did the trick, beating the hometown nine by a 5-3 score. On the mound for the visitors was one Merv Kline, a sharp-throwing southpaw with a bagful of assorted pitches and pin-point control. Relying heavily on a good sinker when he got into trouble, Kline did not walk a single batsman in going the route; one of the six hits given up by him was a sixth-inning double by Gipp, who later scored on a tremendous triple by Buck Wester.

On August 20, with Merv Kline and a budding young catcher with the somewhat appropriate name of Mike Buddo in their starting line-up, Laurium avenged an earlier loss by walloping Albion-Wolverine 16-1. Although newcomer Buddo chipped in with a solo home run, it was Gipp's bases-loaded triple in the second inning that put the game out of the reach of Albion.

The final contest of the brief season was played on September 16 at the Laurium Driving Park, with Laurium coming out of it an 8-1 winner over Albion-Gay. The feature attraction of the game was the return of Dolly Gray to the Laurium line-up. This single appearance of the former local favorite, now a star in the Texas League, brought a large turnout of townsfolk who still had vivid memories of Gray's heroic deeds during his heyday with the hometown nine. The highlight of this game came in the fourth inning when, after the hard-hitting Gray tripled, Gipp brought him home with a tremendous two-run homer high over the right-field fence.

The real significance of this last contest had less to do with the game itself than with a piece that appeared in the sports page of the *Daily Mining Gazette* of August 21. After announcing that the game would be played on September 16, the article concluded with the following information: "A list of 42 acceptances was announced by the Laurium Draft Board yesterday and includes sufficient number of ballplayers to make up a good team. Among the well-known local stars taken are Albert Borgenson, George Gipp, Kurick Tornquist, and Fred J. Wester."

On Friday, September 21, a South Shore passenger train, crammed full with Army inductees, left the Copper Country at 8:00 A.M. for Battle Creek, Michigan. Curiously, as the big train chugged out of the Calumet station, George Gipp was not on board.

Meanwhile, the Notre Dame football team, which observed rules set by the Big Ten Conference, was already well into its fall practice schedule, having begun the first week in September. On September 25 the following item appeared on the sports page of the *South Bend Tribune*: "The team is waiting the arrival of George Gipp, sophomore halfback. Both Harper and Rockne presume, at this time, Gipp must be in the Army."

A fortnight later the Gold and Blue opened their 1917 football season against Kalamazoo College at Cartier Field, at which time Gipp was still missing. A week later, on October 13, Notre Dame battled powerful Wisconsin to a 0-0 tie at Madison. With Gipp still absent, Maurice "Clipper" Smith and Norman Barry were called upon to share the left halfback duties.

Finally, on the Sunday night following the scoreless contest with the Badgers, George Gipp arrived at South Bend, dressed in civilian attire and offering, according to one observer, little in the way of an explanation for his protracted absence.

Just where George had been during this three-week period remains one of the major mysteries of his life. Merv Kline, who received his physical examination at Battle Creek at the time Gipp was supposedly called up, does not recall seeing George on that particular day. Still others insist that George did in fact leave town around this time but that he left for

South Bend and not Battle Creek. Gipp's eventual arrival at Notre Dame has, of course, proved them correct. However, judging by the time it took him to get there, we would have to assume that he walked all the way.

Upon his return to Notre Dame, George, expressing a mild interest in the liberal arts, let himself be enrolled in the College of Arts and Letters. He transferred from Brownson to Sorin Hall, one of two halls that catered to varsity athletes (the other was Corby). His roommate at this time was Walter Miller, varsity fullback and one of several dozen football players who occupied the cellar floor of the building, known to students as "Sorin Subway" because all of its twelve rooms were eight feet underground.

According to Frank X. Rydzewski, then the most celebrated footballer on campus, George loved to come over to his room nightly and sit around listening as the group discussed such varied interests as women, school life, finances, and football. The hours spent in this way contributed greatly to the more relaxed manner George was to display in his second year at South Bend. Also, the past summer had had an agreeable effect on him. Outwardly he seemed to be in excellent physical condition. His robust good health manifested itself in his face, as evidenced by the 1917 team photograph, easily the best picture ever taken of Gipp. He had managed to put on a little weight over the summer, reaching an apex of 186 pounds. The facial pallor that had marked his appearance since childhood, a pallor some were unkind enough to hint was a mark of time wasted inside smoke-filled poker rooms, was gone, buried beneath an even summer tan. Proving that looks are not always deceiving, Gipp reported for football practice the day after his arrival, at which time he informed both Harper and Rockne that he was ready to play.

Seeing a moleskin-clad George Gipp limbering up on the

sidelines that Monday afternoon must have been a sight as reassuring to Jesse Harper as a crepuscular red sky to a weary seaman. In preceding weeks Harper had had more than his share of early-season headaches, most of which originated from problems with his backfield. Several weeks prior to the season's opener against Kalamazoo, Harper had been hit with the disquieting news that one of his star halfbacks, one he was counting on almost as much as Gipp, would be lost for the season. Worse, for the duration. Arthur "Dutch" Bergman, the second of three talented brothers who had come from Peru, Indiana to star on the gridiron for Notre Dame, had been beguiled by the faint roll of distant drums and had responded by enlisting in the Army. One of the best broken-field runners in the Midwest and the man Rockne called "the fastest 40-yard man in the world," Bergman was sorely missed by Jesse.

To make matters worse, Leonard "Pete" Bahan, who, like Gipp, could do just about everything with a pigskin, was plagued with recurrent leg and shoulder miseries. This made Jim Phelan and Walter Miller the only two experienced performers in the backfield. Neither of them had shown anywhere near their potential in the first two games of the season. With the return of Gipp, Harper hoped that Notre Dame would start back on the winning trail. And Gipp's return could not have come at a better time, for next up on the Notre Dame schedule was mighty Nebraska.

On paper, at least, the Fighting Irish were every bit as good on defense as the mighty Cornhuskers. The formidable front wall that had blanked Kalamazoo and Wisconsin on successive Saturdays was led by Frank Rydzewski, the towering six-foot-one, 214-pound center who had been picked in a pre-season poll as a sure bet for All-American honors. Flanking the Chicago-born center on the left were Dave Hayes at end, Frank "Bodie" Andrews at tackle, and team jokester Clyde Zoia at guard. To Rydzewski's right were sure-fingered end Tom King from Louisville and Dave Philbin, considered by many to be the best right tackle yet to play for the Irish. Edward "Slip" Madigan, as thin and supple as a whip, had come over from Ottawa, Illinois to play right guard for Notre Dame.

Some of the credit in the development of this formidable forward wall must be given to assistant coach Rockne, but the preponderance of the credit belongs to Jesse Harper. The lean, bespectacled head coach looked like he belonged in just about any profession other than coaching. Despite his appearance, however, the Irish mentor had a profound knowledge of the game, along with some revolutionary ideas on how it ought to be played. Born in Pawpaw, Illinois, Jesse played his collegiate football at the University of Chicago under the venerable Amos Alonzo Stagg, who according to Rockne got his immense knowledge of the game from God himself. Graduating in 1906, Harper went on to coach at Wabash College in Crawfordsville, Indiana.

At Wabash Harper acted not only as head football coach but as baseball and basketball mentor as well. It was not until he came to Notre Dame, however, that Harper fully demonstrated his ability as a football coach. One of the first things he did was to improve the passing attack initiated by his predecessor, Jack Marks. Although it is not commonly known, Harper has been credited with the design of the first plays to make use of the forward pass. Harper's foremost innovation was changing the pass receiver from a stationary mark down field to an elusive, quick-moving target.

Although his revolutionary passing game was Harper's forte as a coach, it was not the only aspect of the game in which he excelled as a teacher. Like all successful mentors, Harper was a stickler for fundamentals, especially as they applied to defense. He insisted on expert blocking and tackling, and his tactics paid off well. Coming into the 1917 season, Harper's record at Notre Dame was an impressive twenty-eight wins, four losses, and no ties.

On October 20 the winless Irish, George Gipp in tow, traveled to Lincoln to oppose Nebraska. This was to be the rubber match of a series that began in 1915. The Cornhuskers edged the Gold and Blue in the series opener 20-19; Notre Dame bounced back in '16 to win by a score of 20-0.

From the outset, the game was a grueling, nose-to-nose confrontation of superior defensive units, with a slight edge going, as local sports scribes had predicted, to the Leviathans from Lincoln. Early in the second quarter, after two Nebraska drives had been halted by a fired-up Irish defense led by Frank Rydzewski and Slip Madigan, the Cornhuskers mounted another sustained drive that concluded when giant fullback Hugo Otopalik (later to serve as U.S. Olympic wrestling coach) banged over from the 1-yard line for the first and only touchdown of the game. Late in the fourth quarter Gipp, substituting for Smith, broke away on a 30-yard sprint that brought the ball to the Cornhusker 10, but the chance for a tie disappeared after Phelan's pass on the next play, intended for right end Tom King, flew into the arms of Hugo Otopalik. The next day a Lincoln sportswriter, commenting on the 7-0 Cornhusker win, called the Notre Dame defensive play the finest in the annals of Nebraska football. A sadder note was sounded two days later, however, when the Army called up Irish quarterback Jim Phelan.

On October 27 Notre Dame, along with fifteen hundred enthusiastic fans, welcomed South Dakota to Cartier Field. The Gold and Blue came into this, the fifth and final game of a series that had begun in 1913, rated as the underdog. Led by George Gipp in his first starting assignment of the season, the Fighting Irish went on to prove the oddsmakers wrong, winning in a 40-0 romp.

Huron's Carl B. "Rube" Hoy, who played center for the Coyotes that day, had this to say about George: "He would knock you down with a vicious tackle and then, after helping you up, apologize for hitting you so hard."

G. W. "Red" Ellis, who played varsity tackle for four years at South Dakota, still has a vivid recollection of George and the game. "Notre Dame was our big game, and we were all nervous and excited. George Gipp was without doubt the best backfield man I've ever seen. Very fast and difficult to stop."

On November 3 Notre Dame went to West Point to meet the mighty Cadets. The Gold and Blue, subduing the great Elmer Oliphant at last, came out of the fray with a 7-2 victory. The Associated Press pretty well summed up the match, or rather the mismatch, in the following manner: "Notre Dame outclassed Army in every department. They are better coached and better finished. The Notre Dame shift completely confused the Army line. Only in punting did Army have an edge. However, Army is handicapped by a shortage of coaches due to the war. The material on hand is good, but the men are limited to only one practice session per week."

There were two highlights in an otherwise dull Notre Dame-Army battle, and Gipp had a hand in both of them. In the fourth quarter, Joe Brandy was sent in by Harper to replace Tex Allison at quarterback and engineered a drive that carried to the Cadet 5-yard line. In the huddle Brandy called for Gipp to carry the ball over the right side of the line on a power play. George checked the signal and suggested instead that Brandy carry the ball through the middle while he faked the power play over the right side. On the snap, Army shifted to the right, following George, while Brandy dashed across the goal line unmolested. Gipp's strategy impressed an unwitting New York press that, thinking it had been Brandy's brainchild, called the next day for All-American honors for the Notre Dame quarterback.

Late in the contest Army, trailing 7-2, lined up for an attempted field goal that, even if successful, would have been of little help in overcoming the Gold and Blue lead. Suspecting trickery afoot, Gipp hurriedly warned his unsuspecting teammates to watch out for a pass. His suspicion was correct, and George himself knocked down the attempted aerial and saved the game for Notre Dame.

Riding high on their two victories, Notre Dame was off to Sioux City, Iowa, where they met Morningside College at Mizzou Park on Saturday afternoon, November 10. The experts had predicted that this one would be a breather in an otherwise typically rough Notre Dame schedule. The small Methodist college of some six hundred students came into the contest with an unblemished record, having beaten Trinity College 62-7, Wesleyan 33-0, and South Dakota 14-7. Under the tutelage of J. Saunderson, the Morningside line was one of the best in the country and very near the equal, the Irish would soon learn, of mighty Nebraska. The most notable of this formidable foursome was Vic Menafee, considered by many to be the best all-around athlete ever developed in the state. In his first year at Sioux City High School he became the first freshman to win All-State football honors. His coach at Sioux City said of Menafee, "He caught some unbelievable passes under me. Some I'll never forget."

Offensively, the Marooners were led by a hard-driving, unheralded halfback by the name of Jerry Johnson, who, though he ran with his knees high, could do the 100 in ten seconds flat. Johnson, who came into the game virtually unknown to the Notre Dame team, was to emerge that afternoon as the star performer on the field, mainly because he was to have no competition from George Gipp. On the very first running play of the game Gipp took the ball, swung around the left side, and broke out into the open. He traveled 35 yards before being banged out of bounds by Menafee. The force of the collision threw George against a steel stanchion along the sidelines, and he lay there unable to move his right leg. Several of his teammates helped him from the field, and Clipper Smith was sent in to replace him. Taking up a sideline position beside Harper, George viewed the rest of the contest from this unfamiliar vantage point. Nobody, not even George, knew at the time that his leg had been broken.

Horace Wulf, who served in World War I and later attained the rank of General, was the big left tackle who helped Menafee stop Gipp. Recalling the incident as vividly as if it had happened only yesterday, General Wulf said, "We both hit him at the same time and he spun around, his leg hitting a fence post that had been temporarily installed for the game. While he lay on the ground I said to him, 'I'm sorry, boy, I hope it isn't bad.' He replied, 'Forget it, pal, you had to come in, it's all in the game.'"

George's absence undoubtedly hurt Notre Dame. Their offense never got into gear after this sudden departure. The first Notre Dame touchdown came in the second quarter and was the result of an errant Morningside pass meant for Menafee but thrown toward Rydzewski, who snared it and lumbered 20 yards to pay dirt. Another Morningside miscue, a fumble, in the third quarter provided the Gold and Blue with their second and last touchdown in a hard-fought 13-0 decision.

Led by Johnson, the losers managed to outgain Notre Dame on the ground by more than 150 yards, running up fourteen first downs to the Irish's seven. Frank Rydzewski, who collided with a pigskin-toting Johnson more times than he cares to remember to that day, said of the Marooners' star after the contest: "Outside of Oliphant, Johnson is the greatest backfield man I've ever played against."

Gipp's estimation of Johnson was somewhat loftier than that of his teammate. Admitted to St. Vincent's Hospital shortly after the game, George entertained a group of Morningside players who paid him a visit after the game, and said of the burly halfback: "I played against Oliphant, but in my opinion Johnson is the better all-around player."

In all George spent eleven days in St. Vincent's Hospital with a fracture just above the right ankle. Lloyd Scheerer, a reserve center, said that George was always in good spirits when visited by members of the Morningside team. "He had no hard feelings for the boys because of the accident." E. F. Rorapaugh confirmed Scheerer's sentiment when he said, "He was always pleasant and sociable when we visited him."

After his release from the hospital, George took the morning train out of Sioux City, arriving back in South Bend that same day, Wednesday, November 21. The trip had been a solemn one for George since the doctor who treated him at the hospital was of the opinion that Gipp was through playing any kind of sports for the rest of the year. This untoward medical prognosis, plus his inability to navigate properly, upset George greatly. One day after he returned to South Bend, he dropped out of school and, after spending a week in South Bend at the Oliver Hotel, returned home to Laurium. George was still having his problems with his leg in late December, according to Hunk Anderson, who, at Christmas time, remembers seeing George hobbling around town on crutches.

7.

Rockne Takes Over

THE Selective Service Act that was passed on May 19, 1917, required all males between the ages of twenty-one and thirty to register for the draft. Later the age limit broadened to include all males between the ages of eighteen and forty-five. This change in the age limit hit hard at higher education, which was still reeling from the wallop it received from enlistments concomitant with the declaration of war. While all of the universities were feeling the revenue bite from lost tuitions, many of the smaller institutions, whose histories were marked by a struggle for solvency, found themselves on the brink of financial ruin.

Notre Dame, with its all-male student body, was one of the hardest hit, especially in its sports program. In fact by the time George returned to South Bend after his ten-month sojourn at home (December to September), many of the faces most familiar to him were no longer at the university. The broken bone in George's right leg had mended nicely, but it looked as if he might not get a chance to test it on the football field. For Notre Dame, like many other colleges, was at this point seriously considering discontinuing football for the duration. As one school administrator said, "Between the Army and graduation, we just don't have enough experienced players left to even bother about football."

Most notable among the missing was Gipp's friend, Frank Rydzewski. The big, blue-eyed bull had graduated the previous spring, but not before he had been chosen as the number-one center on both the NEA and INS All-American teams. This pair of honors must have evoked a smile on the face of Father Gene Burke when he remembered that day back in 1914 when the big, raw kid came to see him at Chicago's Auditorium Hotel and told him how badly he wanted a scholarship to Notre Dame.

Also missing from the great forward wall that had yielded only one touchdown in helping the Fighting Irish post a season's mark of 6-1-1 the previous year were Clyde Zoia, Tom King, Bodie Andrews, and Dave Philbin. Even George's old roommate, Walter Miller, was gone. He, along with Joe Brandy, Slip Madigan, Chet Grant, Tex Allison, and Dave Hayes, had been called up by the Army and ordered to report to OCS shortly before Christmas.

Meanwhile, George, too, was called up by the military. During the winter of 1918 he received notification by his local draft board at Laurium that he was to report for a physical examination on January 31. George reported at the specified time but was not inducted. According to Hunk Anderson, George was still limping noticeably at the time and therefore was given a six-month deferment by the civilian board. Gipp's draft record, set down on one index card, contains only sparse information, concluding with the following line: "Went for physical 1-31-18; was not inducted."

Although George was said to have been limping noticeably at the time of his examination, it is nevertheless difficult
to determine how much trouble his leg actually was giving
him. Hunk Anderson, for one, says that when necessary
George could "limp pretty good." Still others close to him at
that time reveal that George, like many of today's young
people, was strongly opposed to the draft, though not, it
would seem, for the same reasons. George never gave a reason for his objection, but one would suspect, knowing his
emotional make-up, that it was due more to a resentment of
regimentation than to hatred or fear of the army itself. In
any event he was more than a little happy to learn that the
draft board had found him, for the time at least, unfit for
military duty.

Another prominent figure connected with Notre Dame
football was absent from the scene when George returned to
South Bend in September. A death in his family had compelled Jesse Harper to resign his post as athletic director and
head football coach at the close of the previous spring semester. Before departing for Kansas, where he planned to take
over the management of his prosperous cattle ranch, Harper
supposedly urged the Notre Dame fathers to appoint Assistant Coach Rockne as his successor. How much urging was
needed before he was able to convince the school's president
to give the vacated post to Rockne is a matter of conjecture.
According to the unofficial Notre Dame football historian,
Donald "Chet" Grant, little importuning was needed. "Harper did not have to sell Father Cavanaugh a bill of goods on
Rockne," Grant said. "Everybody would have been shocked
had Rockne not gotten the job. That's how assured he was of
getting it without Harper's help."

In any event, shortly after Harper's resignation, Father
Cavanaugh appointed Rockne to the post of head football
coach and director of athletics. By turning over the job to

Rockne two years after awarding George Gipp his scholarship, Notre Dame had unknowingly pulled off its second masterstroke. The force of these two men was destined to thrust the school into the national spotlight almost overnight.

Knute Kenneth Rockne, the tough, fiery little spellbinder with the barrel chest, bandy legs, and battered fedora, had been Jesse Harper's assistant since the fall of 1914. While serving in this subordinate role, Rock, as he was known to players and friends, had been quick to make his presence known. He was an ambitious, tireless worker, possessed of an uncanny knowledge of football, which he combined effectively with a flamboyant personality and a deep understanding of human nature to become, if not the greatest collegiate football coach of all time, the most widely known and respected.

Rockne was born in Voss, Norway, on March 4, 1888. His family emigrated to America shortly after he reached the age of five, and they settled in Logan Square, an Irish-Scandinavian section on Chicago's North Side. During his days as a student in Chicago's Northwest Division High School, Rockne began to manifest an interest in sports that would remain with him for the rest of his life.

Rockne, like Gipp, did not play high-school football. Rock, however, was denied the opportunity because of physical and not scholastic reasons. Standing only five-feet-seven and tipping the scales at a mere 137 pounds, the scrappy little Norwegian, according to his coach, was just too small to withstand the beating he'd be subjected to by his better-developed peers. Like Gipp, Rockne turned to the sandlots to satisfy his desire to play football and baseball. He managed to win a place on the school track team, where he excelled in the middle distances. His greatest acclaim came, however, in his mastery of the tricky art of pole vaulting.

Not content to be known as a runner and pole vaulter,

Rock tried his hand at boxing in his senior year, and his name soon appeared on the fight cards in many "smokers" throughout the city. Despite the punishment of the ring, Rock's simian nose was not the unwelcome gift of a boxing opponent. His nose was broken in a sandlot baseball game when a teammate, after missing a pitch, carelessly threw his bat, which sailed over to where Rockne stood and smashed him flush across the face.

Despite an intense love of learning, Rockne did not finish high school. Shortly before graduation he and fellow members of the track team cut classes to practice for an upcoming meet, and as punishment the team was broken up and its members transferred to schools scattered throughout the city. In protest Rockne quit school. Shortly thereafter he went to work for the government in the postal department, where he managed to save close to a thousand dollars, which he planned to use to further his education. It was his ambition to enroll at the University of Illinois to study medicine. Friends convinced him, however, that with his limited finances he'd have a much better time of it at a smaller school, and in September 1910 Knute Rockne enrolled at Notre Dame.

Rockne was a year older than Gipp had been when he came to Notre Dame, and the discomfort George felt in the company of younger boys also had plagued the seemingly imperturbable Rockne. According to Gus Dorais, his roommate as well as teammate on the football team, Rockne was always threatening to pack up and go home, a threat that, fortunately for himself and Notre Dame, he never carried out.

Like Gipp, Rockne didn't have much money when he got to Notre Dame, and he was forced to take manifold campus jobs, one of which was waiting table. To augment his income he again turned to boxing, fighting in and around South Bend under the pseudonym of Billy Williams. On an amateur level Rockne became a member of the track and field team and later, in the fall, went out for football. He played four years of varsity football at Notre Dame and still found time to act in campus plays and edit *The Dome*. All of this activity had no apparent effect upon him as a student. In 1914 he graduated *magna cum laude* with a Bachelor of Science degree in chemistry.

In his four years of varsity football Rockne had the opportunity to play under three different coaches, and, as he succinctly put it, "I learned plenty." He was fond of recalling how because of one of the coaches he almost quit football for good in his freshman year. Shorty Longman was coach then, and Rockne recalled that Longman believed the key to a winning football team was the size of its players—the bigger the man, the better his performance. After ignoring Rockne for some time (long enough to force Rockne to consider turning in his equipment), Longman gave Rockne his chance. He inserted the five-foot-eight, 165-pound Rockne into the line-up, unbelievable as it may seem, at fullback against Olivet College. The next day the *South Bend Tribune* wrote in its account of the 48-0 victory by Notre Dame, "Rockne was great at fullback, but he fumbled often."

Years later in recalling the contest Rockne said of himself, "I wasn't very good. Several times I caught the ball and froze with it in my hands. And I did fumble often."

The following season an Ivy Leaguer by way of Dartmouth, Jack Marks, became Notre Dame's head coach. One of his first moves was to shift Rockne from fullback to left end. The move was to pay big dividends for Marks's successor a couple of seasons later. Rockne said of Marks, "He transformed us into a smooth, efficient team, and for the first time we were beginning to be noticed outside the Middle West. We were unbeaten in two years under him."

Jesse Harper became Notre Dame's head coach in Rockne's

senior year, and the change was right up Rockne's alley. The forward pass, legalized in 1906, was seldom used by college teams. Only when a team was badly outclassed did they resort, in desperation, to a forward pass, and the pass plays available to them at that time were indeed primitive in design. This knowledge did not bother Rockne or his wiry roommate, Gus Dorais, who, during the summer of 1913, while working at the resort town of Cedar Point, Ohio, spent their leisure hours perfecting pass plays. Dorais, the Notre Dame quarterback, threw, and Rockne gobbled them in.

On November 1 at West Point, New York, their experimentation paid full dividends. In the first of many historic meetings between Notre Dame and Army, the pass combination of Gus Dorais and Knute Rockne completely bewildered the vaunted Army eleven. When the final whistle blew, Notre Dame jogged off the field after handing the Cadets a stunning 35-13 setback.

Upon graduation both Dorais and Rockne were asked to stay on at the university. Rockne, who was appointed Harper's assistant, was also awarded a position on the faculty as a chemistry teacher, while Dorais was made head baseball coach. One of the first moves Rockne would make after he became head coach would be to name Dorais as his assistant.

Chet Grant, who played football under both Harper and Rockne, has vivid memories of those days. Referring to Rockne's days as assistant and his later tenure as head man, Grant had this to say: "We looked to Jesse for the tactical plan and to Rock for inspiration. Then all of a sudden when Rock was in charge alone it was as if he had matured overnight. Here he was, just thirty years old, but he had great wisdom even then. He was growing fast, and we knew it. He always told us to keep our heads up and our eyes open, and he followed his own advice."

The inspiration to which Grant refers was no doubt imparted by Rockne during the pregame fight talks. Even before he took over as head coach, the fiery Rockne was assigned the half-time orations by Harper, and for two sound reasons. First, Harper had a high-pitched voice that had a habit of cracking, much to his embarrassment, whenever he became overexcited. Second, Jesse respected Rockne's natural flair for the dramatic, plus his added knack of knowing the precise words needed to lift the boys psychologically.

Grantland Rice, a lifelong admirer of Rockne, called him the star between-halves orator. "He spoke in a staccato voice," Rice recalled, "and he had an incisive manner of speech that electrified those around him. His manner of raising the pitch of his voice rather than lowering it at the end of a sentence was as spontaneous as it was effective. After one of his exhortations Notre Dame was likely to push out and sweep away the grandstands. One of his best was but one line: 'So this is Notre Dame!' "

Long after he became a national celebrity and a favorite guest at every gala affair he deigned to accept an invitation to, Rockne remained pretty much the same person he had always been, on the outside as well as the inside. He still had a predilection for a grey or blue suit, either of which always looked as if he had not bothered to remove it before hitting the sack the night before. He crowned himself with a battered fedora that became, like that worn by Walter Winchell, a trademark. Even after newspaperman Westbrook Pegler remarked that Rockne looked like "a beaten up tin can," he did little to alter his appearance. However, Pegler's remark had a lasting effect on Rockne, who never forgave the New York columnist for the unkind criticism.

Rockne's immense knowledge of football techniques, coupled with his ability to transmit this knowledge to his boys, made him a master coach. But the eminence he was able to attain in the course of transforming Notre Dame into the most heralded of all college football teams was mostly the result of a dynamic personality and superb moral fiber. The tough little Norwegian was a man among men, the kind of man who, once you met him, you were not likely to forget. He was a charming, forceful man, blessed with an Irishman's gift of gab. He impressed people he met by his great humanity, his profound understanding of human nature, and a childlike willingness to learn. He possessed all of those qualities we admire in a man: honesty, integrity, loyalty, and superior intelligence.

Although Rockne never studied psychology, he was a master of its use. Many a bonafide practitioner of the science could have learned a great deal from following him about. Had Rockne espoused a particular cause, he could have drawn enthusiastic crowds on any street corner where he chose to preach. His own football credo was, in a sense, similar to that of an evangelist. Joe Boland, who until his death announced the Notre Dame football games on the Irish radio network, expressed his coach's belief in these words: "To play hard, to win gracefully, to lose as a sportsman."

When Rockne assumed the head coach's job in 1918, he was much the same man that he would be in later life. His best qualities were congenital rather than acquired. Time affords such a man experience and maturity, little else. In exploring this aspect of Rockne's personality, it might be proper to examine the effect he had on George Gipp up through his first year as head coach.

George Gipp's character was as fully developed as it would ever be by 1918, and many of the qualities that have been attributed to his mentor also were possessed by Rockne's first and greatest star. With George, however, his minor vices were forever getting in the way of his virtues, forcing them to remain, for the most part, in the shadows.

The positions of the two men strongly influenced the way in which each used his talents. Rockne, as a coach, was thrust into a position of leadership and was able to mix his own noble traits with his unique method of teaching football skills, thus benefiting both the minds and bodies of his men. George, on the other hand, was not a leader of men. Nor was he a follower. George neither commanded nor was commanded, and he worried little about his influence on those around him. With Rockne personal impressions were paramount. Consequently, his efforts have been rewarded by a host of admiring biographers, all of whom have stood in marvel of his sterling qualities. But George's minor vices seem to have shocked the flock of newspaper biographers who have attempted to follow his movements on and off the playing field.

This is not to say that George has been a victim of an unfair press or that Rockne was undeserving of the flattering things that have been said about him by his biographers. The point is that the two men were as diametrically different in as many ways as they were curiously similar in others. For instance, the one thing that made Rockne the great man he became was a driving ambition, and this was the one quality George sorely lacked. Rockne knew almost from the start where he wanted to go, and he worked tirelessly to make sure he got there. When he finally succeeded, he relished the glory that came with being the best, as only a man who made it on his own can. George, on the other hand, didn't know where he wanted to go, being content to do his thing more or less on a day-to-day basis, as if to say to hell with all the glory of a high-sounding eulogy. Rockne was quick to discern George's attitude in this respect. Commenting on Gipp's reluctance to bask in the glory of his football achievements, Rockne said, "Becoming a campus hero is enough to inflate any youngster's head. But this boy Gipp had a personal policy of being indifferent to everything."

(Above) The Gipp homestead, where George was born. *(Below)* George's run-ins with the authorities kept him out of sports at Calumet High School.

The Dome

Northland Studio

(Left) A rare photo of Gipp out of uniform, taken on Cartier Field. *(Below)* The main street in Laurium at the turn of the century. Here George exercised his taste for practical jokes and acquired an expertise at billiards.

The Dome

(Above) An aerial view of the Notre Dame campus: St. Mary's Lake, the Golden Dome of Our Lady, Sacred Heart Church, and the residence halls—Brownson, Washington, Badin, Sorin, Holy Cross, Corby, and Walsh. *(Right)* Gipp in a familiar pose, taken before the 1920 season opener against Kalamazoo.

Social life in South Bend centered around the Oliver Hotel, which had an impeccable reputation despite its basement billiards tables. Here Gipp led the Hull and Calnon team to victory in South Bend's first three-cushion billiards championship.

The Oliver's lobby featured paintings representing the four seasons, the fine arts, the four elements, and the Muses of music, song, drama, and dance. Evidently fond of these surroundings, Gipp moved out of Sorin Hall and took up residence at the Oliver.

The Dome

(Above) Sorin Hall during the winter of 1920. Gipp roomed here for three years. *(Right)* Knute Kenneth Rockne shortly after he assumed the role of athletic director and head coach at Notre Dame.

(Above) The Fighting Irish arrive at West Point for their 1919 encounter with Army. Gipp is in the center in the cap and trench-coat. At the extreme left is Hunk Anderson. *(Left)* Gipp ready for practice at Cartier Field.

The 1918 Notre Dame team, which compiled a record of 3 wins, 1 loss, and 2 ties.

WESTERN CHAMPIONS 1919

The Fighting Irish played to the Western Championship in 1919. Gipp stands at top row center to the left of his friend Hunk Anderson. Rockne is at far left, Gus Dorais at far right.

(Above) Gipp picks up 15 on a power play over left tackle against Nebraska at Lincoln, 1919. (Below) Gipp poses for a photographer shortly before taking the field against Purdue.

HALFBACK
IRISH VICTOR

The Dome

(Above) Gipp watches the first-quarter action against Valparaiso. In this game Rockne started his second unit, an unheard-of maneuver. *(Below)* Gipp (center) races in to assist tackle Maurice Smith in stopping the Cornhusker ball-carrier for no gain during the 1919 encounter with Nebraska.

MacDonald Studio

CALUMET-LAURIUM BASEBALL TEAM
UPPER PENINSULA CHAMPIONS 1919
WINNERS OF COPPER COUNTRY LEAGUE CUP 1919

Gipp helped make the Calumet-Laurium baseball team champions in 1919. Gipp is at middle row right; manager Joe Swetish is next to him.

Cartier Field on Notre Dame's first Homecoming Day, November 6, 1920. The Irish
took on Purdue before 12,000 spectators.

(Left) Football savants expected the 1920 Notre Dame-Army match to be a contest between Gipp and Army backfield star Walter French. *(Below)* Rows of sober-faced cadets watch as Notre Dame, led by the irrepressible Gipp, puts an end to their hopes for an undefeated season.

The Dome

A view of the 1920 Nebraska game; Gipp's passing led Notre Dame to victory 16—7.

Gipp entered St. Joseph's Hospital early Tuesday morning, November 23, 1920. He complained of a sore throat and chills. After a three-week illness, Gipp died on December 14.

The George Gipp monument in Laurium, Michigan, dedicated August 3, 1934.

Just as he was quick to note a dissimilarity in their objectives, Rockne was every bit as quick to take notice of something each of them had in common. After he had gotten to know George fairly well, sometime after the latter had won a berth on the varsity team in 1917, Rockne said, "The lad has brilliance and a sense of opportuneness of doing the right, unpreconceived thing at exactly the right, unpreconceived moment that makes me wonder, at times, what self-dramatizing leaders of men must have been among his forebears." Unfortunately, we do not know what prompted this observation or to whom it was made, but we do know that Rockne judged George's dramatic flair as almost equal to his own. We know, too, that Rock was impressed with George's intelligence. Himself a man with an incisive mind, Rockne invariably took note of this quality in other men he met, and George was not an exception. "The boy had unmistakable class," Rockne said. "I was convinced after the incident in the Army game of '17 when George knocked away the pass that he had a head on his shoulders. That was quick thinking." Perhaps with a portent of trouble ahead, Rockne concluded, "I knew there'd be nothing to stop this man being the outstanding star of his next full season. Nothing, that is, except Gipp."

George's humor also impressed Rockne. The Notre Dame head man admired anybody with a quick wit. Rockne himself could be witty on occasion, but his humor usually was of a sardonic nature. After learning of the incident that involved Gipp's quip about cleanliness and Godliness, Rockne laughed uproariously. He commented later: "This hallmark of humor just stamped him—at least in my sight—as the solid gold article called greatness."

Of course, much of the affection Rockne had for George arose out of respect for Gipp's talent. Years later, when recalling his discovery of George on that fall afternoon back in '16, Rockne said, "Forgive me for speaking in this proprietary, or at least paternal way of the boy, because I felt the thrill that comes to every coach when he knows it is his fate and responsibility to handle unusual greatness—the perfect performer who comes rarely more than once in a generation."

It is doubtful that George had any filial response to the father image affected by Rockne. For one thing the closeness of their ages would not permit it. Furthermore, one didn't come out of the harsh environment of a copper mining town searching for a surrogate father. By the time George was sixteen he already was able to take care of himself in the manner befitting an independent man. Yet something about Rockne moved George emotionally; if not his dynamic personality, it was the direct, honest approach he always used in dealing with George. From the beginning the two felt a mutual respect that was the basis for a unique rapport. Their rapport sometimes even showed signs of developing into a solid friendship. We know that George was entertained by Rockne and his charming wife, Bonnie, on frequent informal visits to their modest home on South Bend's St. Vincent Street.

This is not to say that the relationship between Rockne and Gipp was as placid as the lull before the storm. Quite the contrary—there were at least as many storms as there were lulls. From the outset George stubbornly resisted the Rockne charm that had cast a benign spell over close friends and players alike. George also resisted Rockne's authority as head coach. This obstinacy often had damaging repercussions for both men, though in the beginning it was Rockne alone who suffered greatly.

From the very beginning Rockne expressed concern over George, mostly because of the latter's love of gambling. Although it afforded George the opportunity to quit waiting table at Brownson Hall after only one semester, the gambling cut a sizable swath from the time that should have been reserved for study. Even though Gipp somehow maintained passing grades, thanks to a remarkable ability to cram on the

night before an examination, Rockne was less than satisfied. In recalling 1918 Rockne noted, "When he came back
that fall he switched his course from the arts to law, which
meant nothing to me so long as he studied."

In recent years a number of writers have reported that
George's gambling caused Rockne most of the woe he experienced in his first year as head coach. These writers have
cited Gipp's frequent absence from practice sessions, as well
as his reluctance to work out in the manner prescribed by
Rockne beforehand: George, the story goes, instead of
scrimmaging with the team, preferred to stand along the
sidelines, occasionally tossing a pass or practicing drop kicks.
What these writers have failed to take into consideration is
that George had come back to school that fall with a recently
mended leg that was as yet untried. For this reason alone we
must accept Hunk Anderson's statement that George only
missed practice sessions on those occasions when his leg was
bothering him. What makes Anderson's statement all the more
believable is the knowledge that George's leg gave him
trouble for the remainder of his brief life. In fact in an effort
to protect the leg from unnecessary punishment by a blood-
thirsty opponent, George cleverly took to taping both legs
before each game in order to add an element of confusion.

Another charge made against Gipp at this time does bear
some truth—other players were taped, suited up, and on their
way to the practice field before George wandered into the
locker room. That George was inclined by nature to be dila-
tory is revealed by his baseball teammate, Joe Savinni: "Often
before one of our Sunday games we would have to send a
kid over to Gipp's house to try to make sure George got to the
field in time for the start of the game. Sometimes the poor kid
would stand in the front yard for ten minutes, yelling his
head off, before he was able to wake George. After that the
kid would sit on the front steps for another half hour before
George came downstairs, dressed and ready to go to the park.

Usually we were ready to start the third inning by the time George got there."

Seconding Savinni's recollection of Gipp's tardiness is a former teammate of George's at Notre Dame, who recalls that Assistant Coach Gus Dorais was sometimes sent to Sorin Hall by Rockne when George was late for a practice drill.

For all of his early headaches with George, which included often catching him hiding behind a tree smoking a cigarette when he should have been limbering up with the rest of the players, Rockne was nevertheless counting heavily on his star halfback.

"In his first year of gridiron play we held him under leash," Rockne said. "We had plenty of stars and he was only twenty-two and the war was on, and it was my policy to save him for the 1918 season. At that time it looked as if all of our first-string men would join the service."

When 1918 finally arrived Rockne's fear was realized. All of his stars were indeed engaged in a more deadly kind of combat. We cannot be sure if George knew that the hopes of the Fighting Irish were to rest on his broad shoulders come the next season, but we do know that he shared Rockne's concern for a lack of suitable manpower.

One evening during the summer of '18 George bumped into his old friend of high-school days, Frederic Larson, on a Calumet street. "What's your plans for the future?" George asked.

"I plan to join the Army," Larson replied.

"Come down to Notre Dame and play football," George said. "If we don't kill you by the time the season is over, then join the Army."

Later he made the same proposition to another friend, Hunk Anderson, and as we shall see, Notre Dame was soon to profit twice more from talent spawned in the Upper Peninsula of Michigan.

8.

The Season That Almost Wasn't

Heartly William "Hunk" Anderson, the second man George Gipp recommended to Rockne for a scholarship in the fall of 1918, was a young man endowed with the traits of daring and raw courage that seem to be the birthright of all those of Scotch-Irish ancestry. Had he been born some forty years sooner and several hundred miles farther west, Anderson might easily have taken a rightful place alongside Wyatt Earp and Doc Holliday. Many of the qualities that set these two men apart from the rest of their contemporaries belong also to Anderson.

Like Earp and Holliday, Anderson had a brilliant, facile mind, and his manner, like theirs, was honest, direct, and often deliberately gruff. He hid a strong underlying current of compassion that was easily brought to the surface by any sincere appeal. Measuring an inch shorter than Earp and outweighing Doc Holliday by some forty pounds, Anderson

89

was one of those men who have iron deposits where most men have only muscle. And like those two celebrated figures of the Western frontier, Anderson could be more than a match for anyone when it came to a fight. His close friend, Grantland Rice, once said that he was "tougher than saddle leather at 170 pounds."

The son of a railroad yardmaster, Hunk was born in Tamarack, a small, bleak, copper mining village outside Calumet. Later the family moved to nearby Hancock, and Hunk, like Gipp, attended Calumet High School, where he was an all-sports performer, starring in baseball, basketball, football, and hockey. In his senior year his brilliant performances on the gridiron earned him the coveted fullback berth on the All-State scholastic team. After graduation in the winter of '16, Hunk, though he craved higher education, was forced by family circumstances to go to work instead.

After a brief stint as a streetcar conductor, Anderson acquired a position as chauffeur for Skiff Shelton, a prominent executive of the C&H Mining Company. Meanwhile, Hunk kept alive his interest in sports by playing semi-pro baseball and football around his hometown. During this time he gained a reputation throughout the Upper Peninsula as a rugged amateur boxer. Like "The Great White Hope," Jim Jeffries, Anderson was tough: thick-skinned, with heavy bone structure, which gave him a high threshold of pain and enabled him to take a punch. Powerfully built, with square shoulders and massive arms and fists, Hunk's own punch was as stunning as a slaughterhouse sledge hammer. These physical attributes, plus unflinching courage, made Hunk one of the best amateur fighters in Michigan history.

He was still very much active in the ring and on local sandlots when the opportunity to attend Notre Dame suddenly came his way in the fall of 1918. Hunk had this to say about the events that led to a scholarship for him: "One night Gipp got together with Dolly Gray and Fred Larson to talk about scholarships. Gipp and Gray decided on Larson first, and he left for South Bend in late August. Gipp told me, 'I'll go down and talk to Rock, and if everything works out I'll get in touch with you.' Gipp got to Notre Dame on a Tuesday and sent me a wire that same night. In it he said, 'Come on down, everything's all set.' I told my boss, Shelton, that I was leaving because I had a chance to get a free education, and he said, 'Go ahead, it's a good thing.' He gave me my pay, which was $100 a month, and another $100 extra. I took the electric train over to Calumet and spent the whole afternoon getting my teeth fixed. That same night my father got out a little red wagon and put in my suitcase—a steamer trunk—and my sister's trunk (she was going back to Marquette Normal where she was studying to be a school teacher), and with me pulling the wagon the three of us walked to the depot a mile and a quarter away."

Arriving at South Bend, Hunk was met at the train station by George. Together they strolled over to Michigan Street, where they ran into Knute Rockne, who happened to be standing on the sidewalk outside of Hullie and Mike's, then a favorite gathering place of Notre Dame men.

Aware of Notre Dame's need of linemen, Gipp said to Rockne, "Hunk here is ready to play, and anyplace you play him will be jake."

"George tells me you want to play football," Rockne said.

"That's one of the reasons why I'm here," Hunk replied.

Once on campus George offered his hometown buddy a piece of sage advice. "Listen, Hunk, you've got a lot of friends down here, but when you get inside that green fence you knock whoever's standing in front of you on his ass."

Once inside Cartier Field, Hunk proved he was a man who heeds good advice. "I knocked Rock on his ass six times trying to show me something." This was a classic example of the young Hunk Anderson, whose motto at Notre Dame became as well known as it was simple and direct: "We'll do the best I can."

Meanwhile, Frederic Larson, better known in the annals of Notre Dame football as Ojay (a sobriquet tagged on him after he displayed a campaign poster on the wall of his dormitory room of an uncle by that name who ran for and won a seat in the Minnesota legislature), had already settled in at the school. Larson was sharing a room with his recent benefactor, George Gipp, in Sorin Hall, an arrangement that led Larson to remark that George was the fastest reader he had ever seen in his life. Larson no doubt witnessed that faculty on those nights when George burned the midnight oil cramming for examinations the next day.

Ojay was born in Laurium, attended Calumet High School, and starred at center on the football team for three seasons. A tall, rangy kid who stood six-feet-one and scaled a solid 185 pounds, Larson was quick and well coordinated, which helped make him a smooth-fielding first baseman on the school baseball team. In his senior year he tried out for basketball and developed into a fine running guard. After graduation in 1916 Larson went to work in Lake Linden in the bleaching factory of the C&H. In his spare time he participated in amateur and semi-pro sports, playing football in 1917 for his local YMCA team and later starring on a local hockey team. Like his friend Hunk Anderson, he came to South Bend hungering for a college education, and what's more, like Anderson, he showed enough in preseason scrimmages to earn a place on the Fighting Irish's first team.

In looking back on this time both Larson and Anderson agree that among the first- and second-year men, George Gipp was the main topic of conversation. Their observations match those of other freshman candidates that year, including Roger Kiley, who came to South Bend after graduating from

St. Philip's High School in Chicago: "I wasn't good enough to make the team, even though freshmen were eligible, but was on the freshman team that scrimmaged some with the varsity. But I never got close enough to our hero. In the spring I had grown some in weight and confidence and gave a pretty good account of myself—so much so that one night in South Bend after I had an especially good afternoon, I met George on the street and he said, 'Hello, Roge.' I went right out and wrote my mother about this great event. This is not exaggerated—it indicates the awe in which George was held."

Another candidate, Indiana's Harry Mehre, was equally impressed with Gipp even before he had seen either George or Notre Dame. "We looked up to Gipp. He was older and more mature. Back home the priests shoved me a little towards Notre Dame, and I'm sure my mother would have perished if I didn't go to a Catholic school. But it was after reading about Gipp and Bahan, especially Gipp, in the 1917 Army game that made me want to play in an Army game with Notre Dame."

Meanwhile, George found that the transition from Harper's to Rockne's style of football was not particularly difficult. Rockne was a product of the Harper school of football, and this led to many similarities in their styles. In the beginning at least Rockne stayed pretty much with the Harper system, a style of football that stressed fundamentals and developed teams that were well versed in blocking and tackling. This probably accounts for Rockne's later obsession with blocking and his respect for men who were good blockers. One of Rock's favorite exhortations during workouts was, "Knock 'em up into the nickel seats." Later, of course, Rockne's innovations developed into the more popular Notre Dame style of play, described by him in the late twenties: "I have a basic type of football which stresses deception and getting the jump on the other fellow."

In the word "jump" Rockne undoubtedly made reference to speed. According to Harry Mehre and a slew of other ex-Notre Damers who played for Rockne, speed was the big asset, a fact illustrated in 1924 when the Irish mentor turned a galloping quartet of flyweights into the Four Horsemen. By "deception" Rockne obviously meant the famous Notre Dame shift. A popular belief holds that the shift, a maneuver by the backfield that often baffled the opposition, was a Rockne original. The truth is that Rockne got it from Harper who got it from Stagg, and where Stagg got it is anybody's guess. Rockne's basic contribution to the shift was his polishing of it; he never took credit for the shift's origin. In fact he once issued a statement in an effort to dispel the notion that he had fathered it.

According to Rockne, after Notre Dame went to New Haven and absorbed a 28-0 drubbing at the hands of Yale, Harper decided that he had to come up with a sparkling innovation in their offense. After mulling over several ideas, he settled for a shift that resembled the one used by Stagg at the University of Chicago when Harper was a substitute quarterback there. Harper's shift differed from Stagg's in that it was designed to cover twice the territory. Also, in his original plan Harper wanted the whole line to shift, but after several practice sessions he decided to let the line remain stationary. Rockne's contribution came later when he made the ends shift in and out of a stationary line.

Gus Dorais had a slightly different opinion of the origin of the shift, which he claimed came to Notre Dame from Dartmouth by way of Jack Marks. According to Dorais, Marks, in 1911, introduced the box formation at South Bend, a move that initiated the Notre Dame style of play. Later Harper varied Marks's pattern slightly, and still later Rockne made the ends shift with the backfield.

Long after Rockne's innovation changed much of the

Harper-style offense, one particular play remained in the Gold and Blue arsenal. It was known to the players as Number 51, an off-tackle running play. It was George Gipp's favorite running play, one that he executed with perfection during the 1918 season. That season, because of the war, was to rank as the briefest in modern Notre Dame football history. In addition the season was marred by a complication of the first order—the dreaded epidemic of Spanish influenza.

In the meantime, however, thanks in part to Gipp's recruiting services and the eligibility of freshmen, Notre Dame and its new head coach were able to field a football team. Even more important, the team would not discredit the school.

When the team traveled to Cleveland for the season's opener against Case Tech on September 28, the starting lineup was as follows: Bernie Kirk and Eddie Anderson at ends; Rollo Stine and Charlie Crowley at tackles; Hunk Anderson and Clipper Smith at guards; and Ojay Larson at center. Sharing the bulk of the backfield burden with Gipp was the veteran Pete Bahan at right half. Native South Bender Bill Mohn barked the signals, and Earl "Curly" Lambeau held down the fullback spot (the same Lambeau, incidentally, who went on to make his mark in football as founder and coach of the celebrated Green Bay Packers).

Hunk Anderson recalls that the Case Tech game was played on an unusually hot late-September day, with the players from Notre Dame having a difficult time trying to adjust to a field whose sandlike texture made the footing treacherous. Apparently Gipp and Bahan had little trouble with either the heat or the condition of the field since they tore through the Tech line almost at will, leading Notre Dame to an easy 26-6 victory. William Edwards, the rangy Tech lineman from Cleveland who had a part in trying to stop Gipp that afternoon, had this to say about the Irish's star halfback: "He furnished the necessary offensive strength to win the game for Notre Dame. He was a very powerful, fast runner who made good use of his interference. And he could run to the right or left equally well. The only way to tackle him was from the blind side. I found the best way was to grab hold of his uniform and hang on until help came along."

Another Tech star, Austin Vanderhoff, was in complete agreement with Edwards: "The more tacklers on hand, the better chance of bringing Gipp down."*

Shortly after the Case Tech game the second of three distinctive waves of an exotic malady hit the shores of North America. Unlike the first wave, which hit in May and was mild in nature, this new wave of Spanish influenza left in its wake tens of thousands of deaths. At the height of its intensity the epidemic forced a ban on all public gatherings and sports events and brought business to a standstill in those areas hardest hit. What made the disease all the more deadly was that it baffled medical science. Even though most of the nation's doctors had been mobilized for war, the number of deaths resulting from the disease was especially high in the cantonments.

The effect of the disease on sports events is graphically illustrated by what took place at Notre Dame during this time. The game against Kalamazoo scheduled for October 12, two weeks after Case Tech, was cancelled. This was followed by cancellations of the Purdue game, scheduled for October 19, and the October 26 game against Camp Custer. Rockne and school officials quietly went to work anyway and arranged a contest with Nebraska that was scheduled for November 2 at Lincoln. The *South Bend Tribune* wrote on

---

*Vanderhoff later spent two years as head football coach of King's College in Bristol, Tennessee. In 1922 his Red Tornadoes crushed Lenoir-Rhyme College of North Carolina by a score of 206-0. The last quarter was brought to a halt after only seven minutes of play because of darkness.

the Thursday before the contest that Notre Dame would em-
bark at 6:29 P.M. Friday on the New York Central. Twenty-
one players were scheduled to make the trip. However, just
prior to train time, the Cornhuskers called off the contest,
and it was rescheduled for a later date. Fin Scott of Nebraska
sent the following telegram to Athletic Director Rockne, explaining his school's sudden action: "Lincoln city council has
voted to keep ban on sporting events in effect because of flu,
even though state has lifted ban."

Rockne went to work and contacted Wabash College that
same Friday night, and by seven o'clock a game between the
two schools had been arranged for the next day. Next morning at five o'clock the Gold and Blue boarded a train and were
off to Crawfordsville to oppose Wabash College.

Coached by ex-Notre Damer Robert "Pete" Vaughan (class
of 1910), the gridsters of Wabash were no match for their
bigger, more aggressive opponents from South Bend, who
went on to win by the humiliating score of 67-7. Gipp's performance in the game is best described by John "Fuzzy"
Ott, Wabash's sterling right guard: "We were badly outclassed. My job was to dive into the interference and grab
legs. I may have laid a hand on Gipp once or twice, but that
was all. He made some great runs against us. He didn't seem
extra fast but enough so when combined with his elusiveness
and strength."

In the fall of 1918 the Army brass, in an effort to combine
education and the training of qualified young men as eventual
officers in a burgeoning Army, established a program known
as the Students' Army Training Corps in practically all of
America's colleges. In this program young men of draft age
were allowed to continue their studies at the expense of the
government while learning combat tactics and leadership
from qualified Army officers. The establishment of the SATC

proved a boon to colleges on two counts: it allowed schools such as Notre Dame to play out its football schedule unmolested by the draft, and at the same time the compensation paid the colleges by the government for the use of their facilities saved them from financial collapse.

Ojay Larson and Hunk Anderson enlisted in the SATC soon after its inception. Their benefactor, George Gipp, on the other hand, was turned down because at age twenty-three the Army considered him too old.

Despite being rejected by the SATC, Gipp made it a habit to watch members drill. According to Ojay Larson, George often watched from a campus walk and would sometimes kid them if they missed a step.

Hunk Anderson has supplied us with a typical day in the life of one of the trainees: "We got up at 5:30 A.M. and drilled till 7:00 A.M., after which we went to the mess hall to eat. After that we went to class. At 3:00 P.M. we went back to the drill field, except on those days when Rockne had us excused for football practice. We wore Army uniforms to class."

On November 9 a splendid service team, Great Lakes, steamed onto Cartier Field to oppose the Fighting Irish. The highly favored seamen's ground attack was led by a former All-American from Northwestern, Paddy Driscoll, while their line, outweighing the Irish ten pounds to the man, was fortified by a trio of ex-Notre Damers: Charlie Bachman, Emmett Keefe, and Jerry Jones.

Before several thousand screaming fans, George Gipp, executing his favorite off-tackle play, spearheaded a first-quarter drive that gave Notre Dame its first and only touchdown of the game. After Bahan's conversion made it 7-0, Paddy Driscoll, displaying much of the running talent that made him an All-American, single-handedly carried the ball deep into Notre Dame territory on a drive that culminated with his sweep around left end for a touchdown. He then booted the point after to knot the score. From that point on it became a grueling, scoreless contest highlighted by spectacular play on the line by Hunk Anderson, Charlie Crowley, Bernie Kirk, and Clipper Smith for Notre Dame, while ex-Notre Damers Charlie Bachman and Jerry Jones did yeomen service for the sailors.

Commenting on the 7-7 tie, Great Lakes coach Captain McReavy said, "I have nothing to say except the Notre Dame backs are wonderful."

A week after Great Lakes, Notre Dame put its unbeaten record on the line against Michigan A&M (now Michigan State University) at East Lansing. In a game that can best be described as a modern-day version of the battle between David and Goliath, the heavier Aggies, taking advantage of a muddy field that slowed up the Irish running and passing game, went on to upset Notre Dame by a score of 13-7. Early in the third quarter, after picking up 52 yards rushing in only fifteen carries despite the sloppy playing conditions, George Gipp was forced to leave the game after sustaining a broken vessel in his face.

"After we lost Gipp we were ineffective," Hunk Anderson recalls. "We could have won if he were able to play the whole game. He was a great mudder."

Meanwhile, the Purdue game, cancelled earlier, was rescheduled, and the two teams clashed on November 23, the outcome to determine which of the two teams would be crowned collegiate champion in the state.

Quarterback Bill Mohn, who played the best game of his career, got the Gold and Blue off to a fast start by romping 73 yards for a touchdown less than two minutes after the start of the game. After that George Gipp took charge, gaining an impressive 137 yards in only 19 carries and chalking up an additional 51 yards passing, leading Notre Dame to a surprisingly easy 26-6 victory.

On Thanksgiving Day, November 28, Notre Dame traveled to Lincoln to finish out its season against the once-mighty Cornhuskers. Playing most of the game without George Gipp, the Irish were forced to settle for a scoreless tie against a team that was one of the weakest in the annals of Nebraska football. Gipp, who had to leave the game early in the first quarter due to the effects of a sore throat, never got the chance to get his team's offense in gear. Late in the fourth quarter, however, Norm Barry and Gipp's replacement, Johnny Mohardt, sustained a drive that led to an ultimate touchdown. However, Barry's 18-yard touchdown run was nullified by the referee, who said that Barry had been guilty of hanging onto the back of Chet Wynne, his fullback, at the time he crossed the goal line.

Here again Hunk Anderson asserts that "had Gipp been in the line-up, Notre Dame would have won the game."

Despite a war and an epidemic, Notre Dame got in a season of football. That they had posted a respectable record of three wins, one loss, and two ties must have been a comfort to Gipp, Larson, and Anderson as they boarded the train at South Bend that would take them home for Christmas. The trip, incidentally, proved both exciting and eventful, thanks to George.

George made a lot of money gambling shortly before they left town, part of which he invested in a Pullman ticket. The remainder went to buy enough bottles of whiskey to fill two suitcases. After the trio boarded the train, George entrusted the contraband to his two friends, who, short of funds, were forced to sleep in their seats in the day coach. Traveling on the Grand Trunk Line from Chicago to Calumet, there was a brief stop at Marinette, Wisconsin, a tourist town that had been designated by the railroad as an inspection station.

"We had the two cases of whiskey stashed under our seats when the inspectors came down the aisle," Anderson said.

"One of them, seeing the suitcases, stopped when he got to us and asked what we had in them. 'Our clothes are in them,' I said. He was satisfied with my answer and went on about his duties."

Back home George sold the contents of both suitcases for a reported profit of $400, a transaction that no doubt helped make it a merry Christmas for him.

9.

From Gridiron Hero
to Billiards Star

With boulevard lights adorning all of the main streets and a population of 71,000, South Bend ranked as one of the Midwest's major cities in 1919. South Bend, situated only eighty-five miles east of Chicago, derived its name from its location on the south bend of the St. Joseph River. The city was the manufacturing center for most of northern Indiana, and as such it offered multiple job opportunities for anyone seeking a change in scene and work in a postwar period of social unrest. Add to this a statement published by the local chamber of commerce right after the war that South Bend was the cleanest, best-paved, and healthiest city in the United States, and you'll have some idea why people from all over the Midwest were flocking into South Bend to work and to start a new life in the months following the armistice.

Like all burgeoning, progressive cities, South Bend began

102

to experience its share of problems with vice during this time, of which drinking and gambling were among the foremost. With respect to drinking, for instance, the city had gone "dry" long before Prohibition. Nevertheless, the speakeasy was as much a part of the city as were the many factories that operated on a twenty-four-hour-a-day schedule. The same could be said of the town's gambling houses, or, as they were generally known, cigar stores. These establishments, all of which maintained tobacco counters in front while jamming their back rooms with as many pool, pocket, and three-cushion billiards tables as possible, were at least equal in number to the speak-easies. More important, the revenue derived yearly from their rear rooms may well have surpassed that realized by many of the city's leading factories.

Among the more popular of these so-called cigar stores were Shafer and Plattner's; McInerney and Warner; Hull and Calnon's; Golden D. Mann's; C. Limperin & Co.; and Jimmy and Goat's Place, co-owned by dapper Jimmy Welch and Eddie "Goat" Anderson, a former big-league ballplayer known about town for his pugnacity. The title of the town's leading gambling impresario would have to belong to Golden D. "Goldie" Mann, who operated four such establishments simultaneously, all within the city limits.

Although Goldie Mann led the field in the number of cigar stores individually owned, none of his stores could lay claim to the title of most popular in the city. That honor belonged without question to Hull and Calnon's, more popularly known as Hullie and Mike's to its many patrons, which included nearly the entire student body of Notre Dame.

Located at 112 South Michigan Street, Hullie and Mike's was similar to other such establishments in that its front room, aside from a tobacco counter, held a lunch and dairy counter. The food served was excellent as well as reasonably priced, but the major reason for the store's popularity can be traced to the personalities of the two men who ran it. Hullie, whose real name was George Hull, was a bright, witty, impeccably dressed fellow, popular with customers as well as with many of the town's leading citizens. Later Hull would use the popularity he enjoyed to good advantage by entering politics, going on to serve for twenty-five consecutive years as a member of the city council. His partner, Mike Calnon, had no such desires, content, as it were, to be a hardworking restaurateur.

The two men first met shortly before the start of the war, at which time Calnon ran a "three-cent" restaurant in the Sterling Building on Jefferson Boulevard.* Next door Hull operated a cigar store, and the two men soon became close friends. This friendship led ultimately to the organization and directorship of the popular Coaches' Association, which they founded jointly. It was during this time, also, that the first official football banquet for Notre Dame, under the directorship of George Hull, was held at Mike Calnon's restaurant. The year was 1914. Recalling the incident a quarter of a century later, Hull said, "Steak, potatoes, bread, and coffee were served at a net cost of seventeen cents per plate."

The partnership of Hull and Calnon was a financial success from the outset, and one of the reasons for this can be ascribed to Knute Rockne, who was one of the store's first prominent patrons. Because Rockne had chosen it as his favorite downtown eating place, the store soon became popular with Notre Dame students. Many of them even entrusted their extra money to Hull, who used it to place bets

---

*As its name implies, everything served at the counter — sandwiches, pie, cake, ice cream, coffee—could be had for three cents a serving. In Gipp's time this type of restaurant was a novelty. Its demise came, as might be expected, with the rising cost of food, in addition to the increased salary demands of the help.

for them on the Notre Dame football team. Recalling their student trade, Hull once said, "Mike and I never lost a nickel on a student. And take it from me, we ran a heavy tab. If they couldn't pay while in college, they sent it along after they went to work."

Though the food and drinks served at Hullie and Mike's paid the operating expenses, it was the profits derived from the back room that made the place a financial success. This lively establishment on Michigan Street lured some of the top poker, pool, and three-cushion billiards players in South Bend.

George Gipp first started to frequent Hullie and Mike's in the spring of 1917, and the establishment soon became his downtown headquarters. The move was strongly influenced by his friendship with George Hull. Hull was an expert pocket and three-cushion billiards player, and matches between him and Gipp often were as exciting as any staged in the parlor. The basis for the two men's friendship no doubt developed out of a respect for one another's talent with a cue stick, but it was to prove to be of a much stronger nature, extending far beyond the limits of a friendly pool room rivalry. The two Georges often were seen together outside the confines of the gaming rooms, and Gipp often was a dinner guest at the Hull home at 910 Vassar Avenue. Hullie's wife, Maude, occasionally became annoyed with her husband for bringing George home to dinner on a Monday night, the day she reserved exclusively for wash day.

Gipp's visits to Vassar Avenue (most of which were not on Mondays) still hold vivid memories for at least one of the Hulls' two offspring, their daughter Virginia. "He was very close to my father," Virginia recalls, "and he enjoyed coming to our home. He was a handsome young man, unassuming and so nonchalant. I was only about thirteen or so at the time, but I could see that he was much older looking than the average college boy and much more mature. He was very shy, as I recall, and not given to dressing up much. He didn't seem to care too much about girls, either. I remember people who were introduced to him at our home invariably remarked later that they were surprised to find out he was really George Gipp."

Although many of the people who came to the Hull residence were surprised to find that the young man they met there was George Gipp, it was a different story at Hull's place of business. There Gipp succeeded in making himself instantly recognizable as a result of his stunning victory over a Chicago pool shark known only as "the Greek." The Greek was brought to town by Frank Rydzewski, who was again living in Chicago and starting on a career as a professional football player that would lead to a six-year stint with the Chicago Bears, eventually earning him the top salary of $150 per game. The victory over the imported hustler established Gipp as the number-one pool player in the city. What's more, because of George's easy, laconic manner and the money he won for the people who bet on him against the Greek, George became a popular figure in a tight little gambling fraternity whose members, like mushrooms, waited until after sundown to sprout.

After his impressive victory over the Greek, George participated in what was billed as the city's first three-cushion billiards tournament. This tournament, held in May, catered exclusively to practitioners of the game who played at either Hullie and Mike's or the Oliver Hotel. It was a two-match set played on a home-and-home basis between the two local establishments.

The first of the two contests was played on May 10 at the Oliver Hotel. Led by George Gipp, who played the most exciting billiards of the night, the Hull and Calnon team went on to defeat the Oliver by a score of 115-106. Five days later it was a different matter entirely. Despite a stunning 25-23 victory by Gipp over lumberman Wilbur Sanders, the Oliver upset Hullie and Mike's 114-108. Fortunately, the Oliver's margin of victory was not big enough to overcome its first game deficit, and Hullie and Mike's team took the championship. What is noteworthy here is that Gipp and Doc Beistle were the only two players to emerge from the matches without having sampled the ignominy of defeat.

By virtue of his victories over the Greek and Wilbur Sanders, George became South Bend's undisputed king of pocket and three-cushion billiards. Thus it was that in the days that followed many came forth to wrest those laurels from him. And in the fashion of Gipp, he took on all challengers, beating each and every one of them. Of all who came forth at this time, only one seems deserving of comment here. His name was Ray Fisher, and he hailed from nearby Mishawaka.

Deceivingly graceful for a big man, Fisher, who stood over six feet tall and weighed upward of two hundred pounds, worked for the Ball Band Rubber Company in his hometown. He augmented his salary by giving ballroom dancing lessons on the side. It was not his ability to trip the light fantastic, however, but rather his proficiency with a cue stick that made him a local luminary. During a visit to Hullie and Mike's, Fisher's pool shooting acumen brought about his celebrated match with the formidable George Gipp. Fisher, boasting about his ability as a pool shooter, caught the interest of George Hull. The two got together that same evening and arranged a match in which two games would be played, the first in Mishawaka, the other in South Bend, with two hundred points needed by either man to be declared the winner.

On May 21, the day of the first match, the afternoon edition of the *South Bend Tribune* made the following comment: "The 100-point pocket billiards match between our George

Gipp and Ray Fisher will be watched with interest by local players. It promises to be a keen rivalry, and many local pool experts and fans plan to make the trip to Mishawaka to witness the match."

Just how many local billiards players and fans made the trip to Mishawaka will never be known since the reporters covering the game did not bother to count heads in the gallery. But one thing is certain—those who made the short trip that night were in for a big surprise. Ray Fisher, playing on his favorite table at Matz and Forstbauer's Pool Room, upset George Gipp by the score of 100-91.

The next night, playing at Hullie and Mike's, George came back to knock off Fisher 109-95 and was thereby declared the winner. Thus George eliminated the only man to offer a serious threat to his local pocket billiards dominance.

Soon after George disposed of Fisher he began to expand his gambling activities to include frequent all-night poker sessions on the second floor of the Oliver Hotel. Some say that George rented a room at the hotel around this time, eventually moving all of his belongings out of his room at Sorin Hall. In fact it was not until the following year that George rented a room at the Oliver. Contrary to popular belief, George used the room only on weekends, and not for the purpose of running high-stake poker games for the hotel. George was a loner and did not operate that way. Besides, the Oliver Hotel was not a haven for gamblers during Gipp's time, nor at any other time during the sixty years of its existence.

The Oliver Hotel, like most of its guests, had an impeccable reputation. Built in 1899 by plow manufacturer James Oliver, the hotel became one of the city's downtown landmarks. The six-story edifice, built of reddish-yellow brick and ornamented by terra-cotta architraves, contained 245 rooms and was built in the Italian Renaissance tradition. Its front entrance, situated on Main Street, was sheltered by an iron porte-cochere that extended to the curb, while its side entrance on Washington Street was marked by a dazzling Doric portico. Inside, this same ornate Italian style was carried on in an impressive rotunda, which displayed sixteen beautiful, life-sized paintings of female figures depicting the four seasons, the fine arts, the four elements, and the Muses of music, song, drama, and dance.

A Midwest showplace, the Oliver reached its pinnacle of popularity shortly after World War I. Aside from being one of the most prosperous hotels in the country, the Oliver catered to the upper stratum of Midwestern society. Former employees recall that at all hours of the day and night Packards, Cadillacs, Pierce Arrows, Lincoln Coaching Broughams, Stutz Bearcats, and other such rubber-wheeled symbols of social position pulled up in front of the hotel's main entrance. From these cars alighted elegantly attired ladies hooked in mock helplessness on the arms of dutiful well-tailored men of noble carriage. At night these *bons vivants* sat at immaculate tables in the main dining room amid soft lights and sweet music and sipped fine wine while waiting for attentive waiters to bring them delectable main dishes copied from the menus of the finest Old World restaurants.

Beneath all the glitter and splendiferous living that made the Oliver an aristocrat among hotels there were activities that did not blend too well with the surface grandeur. In the basement, adjacent to the steam rooms, were several rows of pool and billiards tables, put there for the pleasure of those who had accommodations at the hotel. More often than not, and much to the dismay of the management, these tables served instead for men of expertise who came to the basement to earn money from their acquired skills. During its heyday the hotel was headquarters for some of the best billiards practitioners to be found anywhere, including such old veterans as Jack Huston, John Vermande, and Mishawaka's Jimmy Beebe.

George Gipp limited his pool and billiards playing at the Oliver to matches against other experts. One of Gipp's favorite billiards opponents at the Oliver and at the Elks Club was John C. A. Vermande, who for many years was champion of an area that encompassed a part of northern Indiana and southern Michigan. The Gipp-Vermande contests drew some of the largest crowds ever seen at the Oliver and the Elks Club.

Although Gipp worked the Oliver solely to defray everyday expenses, there were occasions when his immense skill at the green tables brought him sizable winnings. George sometimes entrusted to Hunk Anderson's steel locker box as much as four hundred dollars for safekeeping. Unfortunately, the old adage "easy come, easy go" applied much of the time. Apart from George's well-deserved reputation as a free spender, he was also a young man inclined to buck the odds that favored the ivories. At such times vast sums (sometimes as much as three hundred dollars) were apt to be dissipated by a single roll of the bones.

"George was a lousy craps shooter," Hunk Anderson recalls. "I saw him make as many as nine passes in a row and then bet it all and lose everything on the next roll of the dice. He just didn't care much about money."

None of the local newspapers publicized George's penchant for craps shooting, nor did they print, in his lifetime at least, any reference to his poker playing at the Oliver or Hullie and Mike's. Yet his extracurricular activities were beginning to attract the attention of people who, as far as George was concerned, would have been far better off had they remained ignorant of such goings-on. One of these people was Father Cavanaugh, the president of Notre Dame.

Like several others in responsible positions at the school, he was becoming increasingly concerned about Gipp's after-school hours in South Bend, especially since they were in direct violation of the rules of conduct that governed the students. That it was Gipp who challenged these rules made it all the worse. The major consideration here, as Father Cavanaugh saw it, was the effect Gipp might have on the morale of the rest of the students, especially those who did not enjoy the eminence brought by spectacular athletic achievement and who were expected to adhere closely to the rules or face immediate expulsion.

Even though the rumor of Father Cavanaugh's plans to investigate and clamp down on the school's most famous student persisted for some weeks, it did not seem to have any outward effect on George. In fact he did not even bother to take his final exams that year.

Despite his seeming unconcern for the punitive measures that might be taken by Father Cavanaugh, George nevertheless found himself sick with worry when the time came for him to pack his bags and return to Laurium for the summer. The cause of his worry stemmed from the sudden death at St. Joseph's Hospital on May 23 of twenty-four-year-old Leo J. Owens, a Notre Dame student from Ogdensburg, New York. According to friends, Owens's death from septicemia furunculosis (boils) greatly disturbed George. For weeks afterwards, recollections of it crept into Gipp's every conversation with friends. Since people with bad tonsils commonly worry that poison might be seeping into their bloodstreams, no doubt the nature of Owens's death was the primary reason for George's somewhat morbid concern. And since the student's death came so close to the time college let out for the summer, we can only assume that thoughts of Owens were uppermost in George's mind as he rode the train back home.

10.

Gipp Clicks – Irish 1919 Western Football Champs

WITH nearly all of its young men home from the war, life in the Upper Peninsula of Michigan had returned to normal by the spring of 1919. It had been a wonderful spring, distinguished from those of the past by an unusual hot spell that began in late April and persisted through mid-May. The heat wave was the forerunner of what was to be a torrid summer for residents along the banks of mighty Lake Superior. In short it was a great summer for baseball.

For the first time in four years organized leagues sprang up throughout the area; the local six-team league included the Calumet-Laurium Aristocrats, made up primarily of players from these contiguous towns. Upon his return home George joined the local team, being assigned to center field by his manager, Joe Swetish, a local tavern owner who was making his managerial debut.

Aside from the popularity he enjoyed as owner of the Half-way House, Swetish's chief claim to fame was his much-publicized proclamation that he had been the discoverer of

112

George Gipp. Swetish seems to have based this claim solely on his own word, offering little in the way of concrete evidence to support it. Suffice it to say that George had already been widely respected locally as a ballplayer before he crossed Swetish's path sometime in 1918. Nevertheless, the short, dark-skinned, Austrian-born Swetish did not need to qualify himself solely on the strength of his somewhat dubious claim. Swetish knew his baseball inside and out, and after less than a month at the helm of the Aristocrats he was compared by local fans to that former genius of the Giants, John Joseph "Mugsy" McGraw.

According to a newspaper report, Gipp was expected home from South Bend in time for a contest between the Aristocrats and Lake Linden scheduled for June 8, but he did not arrive in Laurium until a week later. On June 23 he made his first local diamond appearance of the season in a contest that saw Calumet-Laurium wallop Twin City 11-0 behind a flashy three-hitter fashioned by southpaw ace Merv Kline.

On July 4 the red-hot Aristocrats won their third game in a row since the insertion of George Gipp into the line-up, knocking off South Range 8-2. In the seventh inning of the game George thrilled the large holiday turnout by smacking his first round-tripper of the season, a four-hundred-foot wallop that scored two runs ahead of him. What made the prodigious poke all the sweeter was that it came off the Range pitcher who had greeted George's two previous appearances at the plate with a couple of fast balls aimed directly at the great center fielder's head. Needless to say, the three-run homer was all George needed to walk off with hitting honors for the day, not to mention a free gallon of his favorite ice cream, compliments of Charlie Salotti.*

---

*Salotti operated a local ice cream parlor. In 1919 he initiated a policy that entitled a Calumet-Laurium ballplayer to a free gallon of ice cream every time he hit a home run.

Three days later, with Gipp hitting and running the bases like a young Ty Cobb, the Aristocrats avenged their only loss of the season by knocking off Houghton 5-2 before the largest crowd of the season at Hancock Driving Park. They came back ten days later and knocked off powerful Lake Linden to assume undisputed possession of first place. The highlight of the game came in the eighth inning when Linden's Berker, racing at full steam, made a sensational over-the-shoulder catch in deep center field to rob Gipp of what appeared to be a sure inside-the-park home run.

On July 28 the hard-hitting Aristocrats, behind the strong pitching of Merv Kline and Detroit import Tom Foley, swept both ends of a twin bill from slumping South Range by scores of 11-1 and 4-0. Six days later they crossed over into Iron Country to oppose powerful Marquette in a widely publicized two-game exhibition series. In both games George Gipp provided the batting punch needed for victory.

The highlight of the second contest came in the sixth inning when with two out, a man on third, and only one run behind, Marquette's Lamere sent a sinking liner to shallow center. It looked like a sure run-producing base hit. Gipp, who had been playing Lamere deep, came racing in from his position with the celerity of the Los Angeles-bound El Capitan and made a diving, shoe-string catch less than thirty feet from second base to save the game for the Aristocrats.

On August 25 at Caledonia Park, Calumet-Laurium and Lake Linden met again, playing before a huge crowd. Part of the outfield had to be roped off to accommodate the overflow. The Aristocrats put an end to Linden's pennant hopes by trouncing them 10-3. Once again Gipp emerged as the batting hero of the day, twice scoring runners from second and third with line shots that ripped into the crowd in deep left field for ground-rule doubles.

With the league title in their grasp and a record of fifteen wins and only one loss, the Aristocrats traveled into Iron

Country to oppose Iron Mountain in a three-game series that was part of the festivities of the Labor Day weekend. Because Iron Mountain already had copped the Iron Country championship, the three-game set would, as reporters put it, determine the 1919 Upper Peninsula champions.

In remembering the auto trip that took the ballplayers to Iron Mountain, catcher Joe Savinni had this to say:

> Gipp drove the car I was riding in, and we arrived in town about three o'clock in the morning. It was quite chilly, and we stopped off at a greasy spoon restaurant. As I remember we had to wake up the proprietor to get some hot coffee and a little something to eat. While we were eating I happened to pick up a local newspaper that was on the counter, and on the sports page was this article about our upcoming games. The article mentioned Gipp, saying that we were supposed to have a guy who could field like Tris Speaker and hit and run the bases like Ty Cobb. I quickly showed it around to the rest of the guys. I remember George got a big laugh out of it.

Two thousand local fans followed Savinni, Gipp and company to Iron Mountain expressly to view the first game of the series. Several of the group promised to wire back the final outcome to the manager of the Laurium movie house, who in turn promised to flash the score on his screen during the showing of the motion picture that same evening. Whether they carried out this plan is inconsequential. The main thing is that Laurium's Chub Eaton, relying on a sharp-breaking curve and pin-point control, hurled his ball club to an easy 12-0 victory. He got a big assist in the field from George Gipp, who turned in several sparkling defensive gems that kept the shutout intact. Offensively, Gipp chipped in with a double and a triple that accounted for 4 of the Aristocrats' 12 runs; Gipp's two-run triple in the sixth knocked Iron Mountain ace Vangoethen out of the box.

Laurium followed up their initial victory with a 4-2 win on

Sunday and came back the following day to win game number three by the score of 9-5. Once again Gipp made the difference. With his team trailing 6-5 at the start of the ninth, one man out and a runner on first, Gipp, before stepping up to the plate, walked over to Joe Savinni and said, "Let's show 'em something this inning."

Stepping up to the plate, Gipp caught hold of a pitch and boomed a long triple that scored the tying run. Moments later he came home with the winning run on a ground single to right by Savinni.

On September 8, in a game that clinched the pennant for the Aristocrats, George went on a hitting spree and led his team to an easy 7-1 win over hapless South Range. In the fourth inning, coming to bat after stylish left-handed swinger Ed Tobola had hit a home run, George uncorked one of his own and put the Aristocrats out front 2-0. He went on from there to collect three more hits, including another home run. His second four-base swat, delivered in the eighth and reputed to have soared over 475 feet, is considered to be the longest home run ever hit at the Laurium Driving Park, possibly the longest in the Upper Peninsula. The home run, coming on Gipp's last official time at bat, was his twelfth of the season and lifted his batting average to an incredible .494, tops in the league. His dozen home runs (in only eighty-three official times at bat) and thirty-three runs scored were enough to put him on top in both these categories, also. In appreciation for Gipp's outstanding contribution to his team, fellow members of the Aristocrats presented George with a handsome leather traveling bag that he put to good use on his trip back to South Bend later that fall.

At a post-season banquet held on Saturday night, September 21, League President Knauff presented Manager Joe Swetish with the customary gold team trophy, and each of the Aristocrats received a monogrammed wool sweater.

By the time Gipp arrived back at Notre Dame, the start of the 1919 football season was less than a fortnight away. That George was late in returning came as no surprise to Rockne. What did surprise the Irish mentor, though, was that George had not come back alone. Traveling to South Bend with him was Perce Wilcox, a hometown buddy and war veteran who had been wounded three times while serving in France with the crack 1st Marine Division. Wilcox had come to Notre Dame in hopes of obtaining an athletic scholarship on the strength of his friend Gipp's influence with Knute Rockne. Only a fair football player (a fact that would be proven in due time), the handsome former Marine more than made up for his deficiencies on the gridiron by his exceptional talent in basketball and hockey. Even though Rockne knew that Wilcox would be of no help to him personally, the genial Notre Dame coach, as a favor to Gipp, used his strong influence with school authorities. Wilcox got his scholarship that same day, thus bringing to three the number of young men who would receive college diplomas thanks to George Gipp.

After helping to get Wilcox squared away, George proceeded to get himself registered, learning at this time that once again he was to room at Sorin Hall. He was to share the room with the amiable Dutch Bergman and George "Red" Fitzpatrick, a scrub halfback who, like Dutch, was just back from the war.

Also back from France and on hand to greet George on his return to campus were a host of prewar Sorin brothers that included Walter Miller, Slip Madigan, Dave Hayes, Cy Degree, Fritz Slackford, Grover Malone, Frank Coughlin, Joe Brandy, and Dudley Pearson, all of whom were eager to resume a safer type of warfare—that of the gridiron.

With Gipp and this host of ex-soldiers returning, Notre Dame had a team capable of demonstrating the Rockne football technique to its fullest, even though Rockne had expressed concern over the loss of three outstanding starters from his '18 squad: Ojay Larson, Bill Mohn, and Rollo Stine. Larson, because of financial problems at home, had been forced to resign from school the previous spring. Upon his return in the fall of '19 he learned that according to Big Ten rules, he would have to be demoted to the freshman squad for one season. Bill Mohn, the promising quarterback, had married a South Bend girl and chose to work instead of returning to Notre Dame. Rollo Stine, the left tackle, never fully recovered from a leg injury sustained in the Great Lakes game; the injury subsequently forced his withdrawal from the university.

Despite the loss of these talented performers, Notre Dame opened its thirty-third year of collegiate football with what many experts said was easily the best team to date. Kirk and Eddie Anderson were at the ends, with Coughlin and Degree manning the tackle posts; Hunk Anderson and Smith were the guards. George "Roly Poly" Trafton, a first-year man at the school, alternated with Madigan at center. Back after a spectacular summer of baseball in Butte, Montana, Bahan found himself in charge of offensive operations as the quarterback. Gipp and Bergman were at left and right halfback respectively, and the hard-running Slackford, after a brilliant fall practice session, got the edge over Miller and became the starting fullback.

On October 4 this highly touted Irish eleven opened its season at home against little Kalamazoo College, coming out on top by the surprisingly close score of 14-0. Years later, in recalling the closeness of the Kalamazoo-Notre Dame contest played before some five thousand partisan fans, Rockne claimed that because of a desire on his part to keep the score down, and in an effort to give Gipp and the rest of the team a strict opening-game test, he had asked the officials to impose penalties on his team without hesitation, sometimes even without reason. He cited two examples to support his claim:

Gipp's 80-yard romp for a touchdown in the first quarter, called back because a Gold and Blue man had been guilty of an offside infraction, and Gipp's 68-yard touchdown run ten minutes later, called back for a similar reason.

At least one individual did not agree with Rockne's version of that particular game. He was Charlie Burlingham, the left guard for Kalamazoo that day. According to Burlingham, the game officials seemed alarmed that Notre Dame might come out of the game with a tie or a defeat, and therefore they took it upon themselves to prevent either of these dreaded occurrences. "Penalties were overlooked regularly when committed by Notre Dame in the late stages of the game," Burlingham said. To prove this allegation he cited a flagrant offensive holding infraction by a Notre Dame player that was purposely overlooked by the officials, resulting in the ball carrier's streaking into the end zone unmolested for the Irish's final touchdown of the afternoon.

Concerning individual performances that day, the Kalamazoo team had nothing but praise for George Gipp. Star running back Forrest "Dutch" Strome, recalling Gipp's 148 yards gained that day, said that Gipp "was one of the best backfield men I have ever seen." His teammate, Miles Casteel, added an interesting note to this account of the game by recalling the following incident: "We had Gipp trapped 15 yards behind the line of scrimmage when he ran to his right. As he was running with several of us in hot pursuit, he kept yelling 'Eddie, Eddie, Eddie,' and then he cocked his arm and threw a long pass downfield intended for right end Eddie Anderson, who had gone down the field to block for what started out as an end-run play. This was the first time anyone had ever passed on the run, and I believe it was from this particular play that Rockne soon incorporated the running pass into the Notre Dame box formation."

Defensive left halfback Lisle Mackay, a superstar at Arthur Hill High School in Saginaw before entering Kalamazoo, remembered the game clearly, and for two good reasons. First, the legendary ex-football great of the University of Chicago, Walter Eckersall, happened to be the referee that day. Second, the game gave Mackay the chance to play against a young man who was rapidly becoming a legend himself—George Gipp. "He was indisputably the most effective of the Notre Dame ball carriers," Mackay said. "He took very long, hard-running strides and was hard to bring down. In fact as far as I was concerned he was impossible to bring down on a solo tackle. Most of Gipp's runs were to my side, and I spent my full time tackling him and hanging on until someone came along to help. I never brought him down once by myself. We all had great respect for his ability. The first tackler to hit him usually got only one leg for a target."

George did not have to wait for the game to begin to impress war veteran John Thomson, a superb runner and passer himself. "When Notre Dame came out on the field, Gipp brought two footballs with him. He stood on the 50-yard line and drop kicked the first one over one goal post, then turned around and proceeded to drop kick the next one over the other goal post. I remember the crowd let out a tremendous roar of appreciation."

One week after the Kalamazoo encounter, four thousand fans gathered at Cartier Field to watch the Fighting Irish take on little Mount Union College from Ohio in what was to be the first and only meeting between the two schools. Ohio college champions in 1918, Union promised to be a good early-season test for the Rockne men. In their season's opener Union had been barely edged out by powerful West Virginia Wesleyan, rated by many members of the sporting press as the fastest team in the country.

Despite some tooth-rattling offensive blocking by Union and a 30-yard touchdown bomb thrown by E. M. McCaskey to his lean, spidery end, Larry Brown, two minutes after the opening whistle, Notre Dame had an easy afternoon of it, trouncing the Ohioans by a score of 60-7. Leading the Irish ground-gainers in the rout was George Gipp, who on the Gold and Blue's first series of downs broke away on a 30-yard run that knotted the score. He came back with two more back-to-back 30-yard jaunts minutes later, the first bringing the ball to the Union 30-yard line, the second scoring a touchdown. In all George picked up 123 yards in only ten carries, and he completed two of three passes for 45 additional yards in the winning effort.

Here for posterity are some comments on Gipp by the Mount Union players. End Larry Brown: "He was a great broken field runner, and we just couldn't stop him." Halfback E. M. McCaskey: "He never once made a gesture that could be interpreted as belittling our little team from Ohio." Left guard Jim Robinson: "He would run to daylight if that were possible, but if he was hemmed in he simply ran over you." Quarterback Earl Marsh: "Gipp was the greatest!"

Notre Dame, which had not scored on Nebraska since the '16 encounter, put its unblemished record on the line against the mighty Cornhuskers on October 18 at Lincoln. The big play of the game came on the opening kick-off when Gipp, taking the pigskin, lateraled to teammate Dutch Bergman, who raced 90 yards for a touchdown. It was a trick play, designed by Rockne and practiced by the team to perfection in the week preceding the contest. That it worked in the game is a tribute not only to Gipp and Bergman but to Hunk Anderson as well. Anderson, seeing that only Cornhusker end Swanson had a chance at Bergman, pulled out of the interference and hit the great Nebraska end with a vicious block that cleared the way for the flying Bergman. Thus Notre Dame ended a scoreless drought against the Cornhuskers that had covered eight quarters.

Bergman's touchdown, plus some fine passing by George

Gipp, who completed five out of eight for a total of 124 yards, was all Notre Dame needed that chilly Saturday afternoon. Despite some brilliant running by a pair of Cornhuskers, Paul Dobson and Floyd Wright, Notre Dame went on before ten thousand spectators to upset the favored Nebraskans 14-9, keeping intact their unblemished record.

That Gipp's passing was in large part responsible for the Irish victory is confirmed by Floyd Wright in his recollection of the game. "In those days forward passes were not used extensively, and it was difficult to complete passes in that the rules required the passer to be 5 yards behind the line of scrimmage when passing. A passer was allowed only two incomplete passes in a series of downs. After that there was a 5-yard penalty assessed for every incomplete pass, and an incomplete pass in the end zone, regardless of the down, was an automatic touchback. None of these rules seemed to bother Gipp, though. He was a fine passer, and because of his passing, Notre Dame was able to get the touchdown that beat us that day."

Saturday, October 25, marked the second time in the season that the city of Kalamazoo sent one of its college elevens to South Bend to play Notre Dame. This time it was the Wolverines of Western State Normal, led by Sam "The Black Streak" Dunlap, a superb black fullback well respected in the West for his power and ability as a broken field runner.

Notre Dame, its spirits obviously buoyed by the win over Nebraska and not the least bit alarmed by the knowledge that Coach Spaulding's Wolverines had trained hard for two months in the hopes of pulling off a sensational upset, wasted little energy in de-fanging the win-hungry Wolverines. The Irish romped to an easy 53-0 win before a sparse twenty-five hundred fans at Cartier Field.

On November 1, amid a steady rain that had made Indianapolis's Washington Park a veritable quagmire by kick-off time, George once more lived up to his reputation as a great mudder as he ran, passed, and kicked his team to an easy 16-3 victory over the Hoosiers of Indiana University.* Gipp, who figured prominently in all of his team's scoring endeavors, averaged slightly better than 5 yards per carry on the muddy turf and was able to pass the slippery pigskin for 57 yards, completing three of the seven passes he had attempted. However, it was Hunk Anderson who once again got the Irish going by his brilliant defensive work, charging in to block John Leonard's punt and thus set up the Irish's first score of the game. In this contest George also kicked the only field goal of his varsity career—a drop kick from 12 yards out.

The following Saturday Notre Dame put its five-game winning streak on the line when the team traveled to New York to meet its archrival, Army, before a crowd of eight thousand. With Gipp and Degree nursing slight injuries that had been sustained in the closing moments of the Indiana game, and with standout Dutch Bergman confined to his bed because of a knee injury suffered in the same contest, New York writers figured the West Pointers were in a good position to pull an upset. And for two quarters it seemed as though the once-beaten Cadets (Syracuse beat them 7-3) were going to do just that. Notre Dame, however, thanks to some standout defensive work by Hunk Anderson, Clipper Smith, and Frank Coughlin, contained the vaunted Army attack and went on to win in a squeaker, 12-9.

Gipp, who despite his injury was able to play most of the game for the Irish, led his teammates' offense with a total of 185 yards, 115 of which came as a result of his completing seven of fourteen passes. In the fourth quarter, with the Irish trailing 9-6, Gipp hit Bahan with a pass good for 12 yards,

---

*The game marked the resumption of a rivalry between the two Indiana schools that had begun in 1898 and was discontinued after the 1908 contest, won by Notre Dame 11-0.

putting the ball on the Cadet 4. On the next play fullback Walter Miller swished over right tackle for what proved to be the winning touchdown.

A New York scribe, writing the next day about the 12-9 comeback victory by Notre Dame, had this to say: "Standing head and shoulders above every individual player on the field was George Gipp of Notre Dame. His clever forward passing turned the tide against the Army. His end runs and stellar defensive work assisted materially in the victory."

Notre Dame made it seven in a row on November 15 by knocking off Michigan A&M 13-0 in the final appearance of the season at Cartier Field. Once again it was the brilliant passing and running of Gipp that made the difference— which, of course, came as no shock to the five thousand fans who watched the game. What shocked at least one person that day, however, was that George had somehow managed to get permission to play in the game. The man who was stunned by Gipp's appearance on the field was John Hammes, the Aggies' hard-driving fullback. According to Hammes, the Aggie coach had learned from Rockne the night before that Rockne did not intend to use George the next day. It seems the last time Rockne or anybody else at Notre Dame had seen George had been several hours after the Army game, after which George had vanished mysteriously. In fact Gipp had not been to school for the entire week and did not return to South Bend until the eve of the Aggie game. As punishment Rockne apparently had decided to have Gipp sit out the game. Unfortunately for the Aggies, Rockne did not follow through on his threat. Gipp, after sitting out the first quarter, came in during the second quarter to pass, kick, and run the slow-moving Aggies into fits of despair.

The following are comments on Gipp by two Aggie players, Brownie Springer and John Hammes. Said Hammes: "I saw many a short pass thrown by Gipp that I couldn't get my hands on. And several times in the game I had a good chance to tackle him, but because of his shifty running, missed him completely." Springer said, "He could run both ends like no other player of his time."*

The following week at Lafayette George put on one of his best passing performances of the year, leading Notre Dame to a stunning 33-13 win over the Boilermakers of Purdue before seven thousand fans at Stuart Field.

In a game that was never close, George took to the air early, hitting on eleven of fifteen passes for a near-record 217 yards and two touchdowns. The first of Gipp's touchdowns came only minutes after teammate Hunk Anderson intercepted an intended Boilermaker screen pass and raced 32 yards for the first score of the game. Despite George's great performance against Scanlon's fine Boilermaker eleven (a victory that gave the Irish its fourth straight state collegiate football championship), the event that made the day for Gipp and company occurred not in Lafayette but many hundreds of miles away in Columbus, Ohio. There, on this same day, an underdog Illinois eleven knocked off the West's number-one rated team, Ohio State, by a score of 9-7, giving the Irish a clear shot at the much-coveted Western title.

The next day Gipp, along with Slip Madigan, Dutch Bergman, Walter Miller, Grover Malone, and a half-dozen other Notre Dame gridders, sneaked over to Rockford, Illinois, to play in a game for which they were paid $150 each. Their appearance in the contest had been arranged by Slip Madigan, who, learning that Purdue players were being hired to play for one of the Rockford teams, suggested that

---

*Hunk Anderson, who went on to a brilliant coaching career in both the college and pro ranks, has substantiated Springer's claim, calling Gipp one of the few players in football history who was adept at running to either his left or his right. Anderson has seen most of the moderns in action.

perhaps Notre Dame men should play for the other. Had any of them been caught it would have meant immediate loss of their football eligibility. Fortunately, Rockford's local press took pains to conceal the identity of the players involved. For the record the team using Notre Dame players emerged victorious.

On November 27 Notre Dame closed its season with nine straight wins by defeating Morningside College 14-6 before ten thousand fans at Sioux City, Iowa.* The game, played on Thanksgiving Day in a driving snowstorm, with winds clocked at forty miles an hour and a thermometer that hovered around the ten-degree mark, was a sluggish affair that never produced a chilling moment to compare with the one provided by the weather.

The Notre Dame team, playing in long underwear and gloves that had been purchased shortly before game time, played one of the worst games of the season, with only Gipp coming out of the fray as an outstanding performer. In picking up a total of 160 yards, 94 on the ground and 66 in the air, George figured in both Irish touchdowns. His pin-point aerials set up Bergman's short plunge for the first, and his long bomb to Bernie Kirk accounted for the second.

The highlight of the Notre Dame-Morningside game came in the third quarter and involved George Gipp. Obviously disgusted with the icy cold weather, Gipp sauntered over to the sidelines midway in the third quarter and stood in front of Rockne.   .

"I'm through for the day."

"Like hell you are," Rockne retorted.

Obviously, George showed good sense in trying to extricate himself from a situation on the field that was, to say the least, deplorable.

---

*A post-season game between Notre Dame and the Oregon Aggies scheduled for Christmas Day was later cancelled on December 5.

Speaking of good sense, much of it was shown later by the Midwestern sportswriters, all of whom picked George Gipp as their number-one back in choosing their All-American teams. Among the more notable of these writers were Walter Eckersall and Indiana coach and football authority Pat Page. Picked along with George for a first-string berth on these two prestigious teams was Chicago's pride and joy, Frank Coughlin.

In the snobbish East George did not fare nearly as well. Although recognized by all the top All-American pickers in that part of the country, the best George was able to achieve was a place on their second teams.

Knowing George, it does not seem likely that he displayed even the slightest concern over the shabby treatment accorded him by these provincial Eastern experts. With George it was the job that counted, not the applause that followed. And nobody knew this better than his teammates.

11.

Problems of a Superstar

On December 14, sixty-five members of the Notre Dame football team gathered in the main dining room of the Oliver Hotel to celebrate their winning the Western championship. The banquet, hosted by the Athletic Association, was a festive occasion that featured Knute Rockne as its toastmaster. Next day the *South Bend Tribune* wrote, "In a gala affair arranged by Rockne and Dorais, which featured plenty of food, jokes, soloists and songs and otherwise catchy strains from a university orchestra, George Hull gave a talk as a loyal rooter of the Irish amid a bombardment of cheers reminiscent of a London air raid."

After monograms were awarded, the varsity men got together to nominate two players to run against each other to determine who would be the team captain for 1920. In a close election that was the highlight of the evening, George Gipp edged out the popular Frank Coughlin by the margin of a single vote.

128

In winning the election George succeeded Pete Bahan as captain. Bahan, despite chronic knee problems that plagued him throughout most of his varsity playing days, nonetheless had been a vital cog in the Fighting Irish's offensive machinery. Come fall Bahan would be sorely missed by Rockne. His passing from the South Bend scene was to leave a void in the life of George Gipp, also, though for reasons entirely different from Rockne's. Members of the same campus clique, Gipp and Bahan often traveled together, their peregrinations sometimes taking them as far as Chicago.

It is doubtful that Gipp or Bahan could have suspected, as they sat in the main dining room of the Oliver Hotel, that fate was arranging one more trip for them to take together. The trip would take them to the fabled city of Flint, Michigan, where motor cars and baseball players were in great profusion during that exciting summer of 1920. The circumstances that were to lead George to Flint were partly in focus at the time of the banquet, as can be seen from an article that appeared on the sports page of the *South Bend Tribune* the day after the football banquet. The following paragraph contains the gist of what was a rather ponderous piece:

> The city billiards contest held at Hull and Calnon's is in the last lap. The tournament will close the latter part of this week. In matches Saturday night, Gipp defeated Vermande, and Beistle won from Baumbach. Both winners made a high run of three during the games.

Four days later, on December 19, a follow-up piece appeared in the *Tribune*:

> George Gipp tied up E. M. Moore by defeating two opponents in the city's three-cushion billiards championship in Thursday's round, held at the Hull and Calnon parlors. He beat

F. Hull 25-24 in seventy-six innings and came back to defeat Doc Beistle 35-25.

The E. M. Moore referred to in the *Tribune* article was Elwyn M. Moore, who roomed with George at Brownson Hall back in 1916. Nicknamed "Dope" by his fellow students because of an almost encyclopedic knowledge of baseball, which enabled him, among other things, to spout the complete statistics of just about every major league ballplayer past or present, Moore was in his senior year at Notre Dame in the spring of 1920. Though he played on the school baseball team, Dope's chief claim to campus fame had been his expertise in three-cushion billiards, an expertise many of his closest friends had the audacity to claim marked him as superior to George Gipp.

Moore's boosters let out a roar that rocked the poolroom rafters when, in the initial match that kicked off the second annual South Bend three-cushion billiards championship, Dope upended defending champion George Gipp by a humiliating score of 35-11. Obviously buoyed by his stunning victory, Moore went on to dispose of five straight contestants, demonstrating what local experts said was some of the finest shooting in the tournament. Meanwhile, Gipp was not doing too badly himself. After his loss to Moore, Gipp, knowing full well that one more such disaster would eliminate him from play, easily defeated such top-seeded stars as George Hull and John Vermande. George came back several days later to knock off Frank Hull and the dazzling dentist Doc Beistle, both on the same evening. His victory over Beistle cleared away the field and earned for Gipp the right to oppose Moore for the tournament title.

On January 10 the pair met at Hullie and Mike's to decide who would be the newly crowned city champion. On hand to witness the match were some two thousand spectators, jammed together as tightly as kernels on a corn cob. Any discomfort they might have endured in such close quarters was duly recompensed by the game itself, considered by all of the experts in the gallery to be the best ever played in South Bend. In the match George Gipp, playing the finest clutch billiards yet seen, overcame a slight lead by Moore and went on to win by a score of 35-34.

An anonymous *Tribune* writer (in all likelihood Arch Ward since his article appears to have been written in the early Ward style) summed up the match by mixing up a bit of football and golf terminology. "Gipp's end runs were effective and Moore's putts were too short, hence we find the former three-cushion billiards champion of 1920."

Unfortunately, George's extracurricular activities were beginning to show. He was gaunt and much paler than usual, which could be ascribed to too little sleep and foul, smoke-filled air. The latter was not mitigated by his own consumption of cigarettes, estimated by many of his friends to have been two to three packs daily. Equally bad was the effect his all-night pool and poker sessions were having on his status as a student. Gipp was given to sleeping late in order to catch up on missed sleep, and he began to cut classes with alarming frequency.

Meanwhile, his perplexed professors were beginning to show deep concern for the campus hero. In a re-enactment of George's Calumet High School days, certain solicitous instructors made it a point to take George aside to urge him to take more of an interest in his school work. Said one of his law professors, "With a little application he could easily have been a *summa cum laude* graduate, and I feel he would have made a superb attorney."

Knute Rockne, reflecting on this same subject one bright fall afternoon in 1920, said very much the same thing in a conversation with his right end, Eddie Anderson. "George

would be the smartest lawyer in the United States if he would
settle down to the books."

With all of his impending troubles, George chose this time
to fall in love. Always reluctant to show an interest in the
opposite sex, an attitude confirmed by a number of attractive
young ladies from his hometown area who had admired the
strikingly handsome Gipp at a distance in his pre-Notre Dame
days, George became more favorably inclined in this direction upon his arrival at South Bend. Occasionally, like many
of his classmates, he dated young ladies of middle-class back-
grounds who attended staid St. Mary's College across the
lake from Notre Dame. Mostly, though, he seems to have preferred the company of several ambitious young women who
belonged to the less-than-exclusive society of South Bend
working girls.

More specifically, there was a rumor rife both in town and
on campus that George had become serious about an attractive young woman who resided in downstate Lebanon.
After what turned out to be but a brief affair, George's attentions shifted to a petite, sloe-eyed brunette of French extrac-
tion who resided in the vicinity of 25th and Central in Indianapolis. There is very little known about this particular
young lady, including where, when, and how she met Gipp.
That she occupied a place in George's heart, for a time at
least, has been confirmed by an Indianapolis classmate of
Gipp's, who on occasion double-dated with the couple. A
favorite rendezvous of the foursome at such times was the
Bamboo Inn, a Chinese restaurant located next door to the
Circle Theatre.

George was still keeping company with this charming
woman when in early spring he met still another attractive
young lady, and this time George lost both his heart and his
head.

From the start their romance was a closely kept secret,
and one of the reasons for this was that she, like the man

whose attentions she encouraged, seems to have been a quiet young lady, by no means inclined to seek notoriety. Their affair was so inconspicuous that, except for a few of George's closest friends, nobody claims to have known anything about it until many years later, long after Gipp's death. The few friends who knew of the woman—all of whom had the pleasure of meeting her briefly—recall her as intelligent, cultured, soft-spoken, and quite beautiful. She seemed poised while giving the impression of being extremely shy and sensitive.

The young woman who possessed these many appealing attributes had been christened Iris and had come from a socially prominent, middle-class family. Iris's father, a devout Roman Catholic of Irish ancestry, was a prominent attorney in Indianapolis. According to several people, George included, the father was staunchly opposed to the romance from the start. Aside from his ingrained abhorrence of protestants, whom he considered heretics of the lowest order, he felt that George was hardly qualified by family background to be a proper suitor for his daughter. Moreover, he was not in the least impressed by the fact that George was famous and a law student at Notre Dame. The father often stated that he was positive that Gipp was not serious about a career.

Despite the father's strong objections, George and Iris continued to see each other frequently, though they took great pains to make certain their dates were kept secret from him. How they were able to keep such knowledge from him is difficult to imagine since in the first few months of the affair George was seeing Iris as many as five nights a week. All of their meetings took place right in Indianapolis, the city, incidentally, about which George once said, "All there is to do in Indianapolis is walk around the midtown circle until you get dizzy, then run home and jump in bed."

Between his dating and gambling George was beginning

to levy a heavy tax on the patience and understanding of the administrators of Notre Dame. He had already become the main topic of conversation among the school's hierarchy when, on March 2, he had decided to try out for the baseball team. George's decision was greeted with great approbation by Manager Gus Dorais. Alas, the possibility of George's bestowing additional glory on the school he wished to represent on the diamond did not soften the attitude of the administrators, who were beginning to take a long, hard look at their prized athlete. Father John Cavanaugh, the congenial president who had been responsible for the athletic atmosphere at Notre Dame and who himself looked upon athletes with great favor, had been elevated to the post of provincial and had been transferred to Washington, D.C. Upon Father Cavanaugh's departure, Father James A. Burns had assumed the presidency. One of the problems that confronted the new president on his first day on the job was the scores of complaints by the faculty regarding George Gipp. Despite his own athletic background, Father Burns was to prove himself a tough, no-nonsense headmaster.

Although Father Burns and certain members of the faculty may have looked upon George as a dark figure beset by gloomy shadows of his own casting, Manager Dorais and members of the South Bend sporting press were looking at the talented athlete under the brightest of lights. Arch Ward, for one, said, "Gipp carries all the attributes of a first-class outfielder. He is much faster than the average man his size. Once George gets under way he is a tidal wave and a Sahara sandstorm rolled into one."

Another appraisal of Gipp as a baseball player came from a pair of scouts who came down to watch an Irish practice session shortly after Gipp joined the team. They had heard about Gipp and wanted to look him over. Aware that scouts from the Chicago White Sox and Cubs would be in the stands,

Gipp approached Hunk Anderson, one of three Irish catchers, and asked, "How about giving me a hint of what's going to be thrown by the pitcher when I'm in the batter's box today?"

"Okay," Hunk replied.

When Gipp stepped into the batting cage for his turn at bat, Hunk Anderson kept his promise. George responded by walloping every ball thrown him clear out of the ball park. Afterwards George learned that he had been highly successful with his deceit. Hunk Anderson said, "The scouts were really impressed with George, and both of them handed him a contract. Both contracts were identical, calling for a salary of $4,000 a year."

Hours later Gipp turned the contracts over to Hunk, who put them in his lockerbox for safekeeping. Later these contracts would be handed back to George under sad circumstances.

Meanwhile, reports of Gipp's behavior could no longer be ignored by the school. On March 8 Father Burns called George into his office and informed him that he had been summarily expelled.

Dressed in a grey business suit that had as many wrinkles in it as there are yard stripes on a football field, sporting a battered hat whose wide brim was pulled down to where it almost covered his thick eyebrows, Knute Rockne, a half-chewn cigar stuck in the corner of his mouth, had just arrived at his cubbyhole campus office when someone burst in with the news that George had been expelled, or, as Rockne had preferred to say afterwards, "fired from the school."

According to the bearer of ill tidings, George was expelled after one of the faculty members had seen him coming out of Michigan Street's Tokyo Dance Hall, a notorious night spot that billed itself as a dance emporium but had a reputation that made it off-limits to Notre Dame students.

Rockne himself, in making his feelings known, put to rest

any suspicion that his star athlete's expulsion had resulted from any disregard for the policy that the school had in effect. "Gipp was kicked out for missing too many classes. It seemed too late to do anything except scold him, and that was profitless. Yet when I talked to him on his remissness and told him that he had put the finish to a brilliant athletic career, he quietly asked me why he couldn't have an oral examination. Townsmen of South Bend even appealed to the school authorities to give Gipp another chance. . . . Gipp claimed that he had been ill, and he got it on that account."

The oral examination that Rockne claims he got for Gipp and that succeeded in getting him reinstated at Notre Dame is one of the most celebrated stories in the Gipp legend. The picture of Rockne walking up and down one of the corridors at the school, chewing away on one cigar after another while his great star sat behind a closed door answering the battery of questions thrown at him by his instructors, is as dramatic a scene as any ever written by Tennessee Williams. Alas, like those created by the great playwright, it is pure fiction.

George Gipp did not have to take an examination. The facts of Gipp's eventual reinstatement are as follows: Soon after Gipp was expelled, the office of Father Burns was inundated with phone calls and letters from irate local citizens protesting the expulsion and demanding that the new president reverse his decision and allow George to return to school. George, in the meantime, after taking his baseball contracts from Hunk Anderson in case he might need them, moved all of his belongings into a room at the Oliver Hotel and, from his own admission, went to work as the house player at Hullie and Mike's.

Twenty-six days after his expulsion, George turned up at Notre Dame again. It was a brief appearance, one that saw him working as an umpire in an exhibition game in which Notre Dame knocked off the Mishawaka Indostructos 8-2.

As we conjure up in our minds the picture of this great athlete, we see him not so much as someone content to act as an unpaid umpire, but rather as a lonely and confused young man, stripped of his right to participate as a player and evicted from the place that had come to be a second home to him. There is more than a hint here that George, so often accused of lacking both concern and emotion, had come to love Notre Dame.

While Gipp waited around South Bend, presumably to be reinstated through the efforts of Rockne, the University of Michigan offered him a scholarship to play football at Ann Arbor under the celebrated Fielding Yost, Rockne's chief coaching rival. This was followed by an offer from Pop Warner at the University of Pittsburgh, which in turn was followed by an offer from West Point at the insistence of its newly appointed superintendent, Douglas MacArthur.

In a day of loose commitments that saw many talented athletes, with little regard for an education, hop from one college to another expressly for the purpose of participating in sports, offers such as the ones proposed to Gipp were not uncommon, nor were they considered to be in any way unethical. Certain colleges delighted in luring away from each other outstanding stars of the day. This practice, along with the coddling of "tramp athletes"—men whose academic careers at certain schools had been limited by choice to the length of a football season—set into motion a lively, spirited competition among colleges. More often than not the methods employed by schools vying for the services of available stars were less than ethical, setting the stage for some of the bitterest of gridiron rivalries, many of which continue to this day.

In the meantime Father Burns shrugged off suggestions that Gipp might be lost to another college, remaining adamant to the pleas of irate citizens. Finally, on April 29, he had a sudden change of heart, and George Gipp was reinstated

with all previous rights and privileges restored.* The reason
for Father Burns's unexpected decision to reinstate Gipp was
a petition sent to him demanding George's immediate reinstatement and signed by scores of prominent South Bend
business and professional people.

On May 8 the *South Bend Tribune*, which had reported
the petition to the public, contained the following article:

> Yesterday the Notre Dame football team concluded spring
> practice. The last practice featured a 7-0 win by the varsity
> over the freshmen. The game featured outstanding play by
> Hunk Anderson and Clipper Smith, two of the grittiest linemen
> who ever donned the Gold and Blue. Bernie Kirk and George
> Gipp watched the game from the sidelines after completing
> baseball practice.

With the addition of George to the baseball team for the
second time in less than two months, many baseball savants
picked Notre Dame as a sure bet to be in close contention for
the Western title.

After making his debut against Michigan A&M, a game in
which he emerged the hero, George was the right fielder in
the next game against the University of Michigan. George
also played on May 15 when Notre Dame knocked off a tough
Valparaiso nine. Six days later against Iowa, however,
George's name was not in the line-up, nor did he play at any
time thereafter that season. Once again he quit the team, and
once again nobody knows why.

In late spring George began to think seriously about an
offer made him by the University of Detroit. Pete Bahan

---

*Frank Coughlin did not offer him the team captaincy, which had been
given to Coughlin after a secret team meeting following Gipp's expulsion. George was disappointed in Coughlin. He told a close friend, "I
wouldn't take it if he offered it—but he should have offered it."

already had accepted a similar offer since it guaranteed him another year of football eligibility. This was not the case with Gipp, however, who still had a year's eligibility left at South Bend. The reason the Detroit offer appealed to George was that at just about the time he received it he had begun to have second thoughts about Notre Dame. For the first time since being called into Father Burns's office, he had begun to feel that Notre Dame had treated him shabbily, and by leaving there and going to Detroit he would be getting even.

On Memorial Day, still doubtful about his plans, George, accompanied by *Tribune* sportswriter Gene Kessler, went down to the capital city to watch Gaston Chevrolet, driving his Monroe, win the eighth running of the Indianapolis 500.

Two days after his return George told friends he had decided in favor of the Detroit offer. A wire sent him by his old friend and former baseball manager at Laurium, Joe Swetish, contributed greatly to his sudden decision.

Swetish had sold all of his business interests in the Upper Peninsula shortly before 1920 and had moved to Flint, where he became the proprietor of a prosperous gambling establishment. Swetish also became friendly with a number of influential officials at the Buick Motor Car Company, which sponsored a half-dozen or more baseball teams in that city's factory league. In his wire Swetish importuned George to come down that summer to play baseball, promising in return to get him a good job with the Buick company. George wired back almost immediately, stating that he was definitely interested in the proposition and would arrive as soon as circumstances permitted.

12.

A Summer in Flint

GEORGE Gipp and Pete Bahan arrived in the
booming industrial city of Flint, Michigan, on June 15, destined to join a working force of some twenty-nine thousand
citizens who derived their living in some manner from its
many factories, which included a giant complex of automotive manufacturing plants that had operated full scale since
before the war.

The two Notre Dame football stars came to town directly
from Detroit, where they had spent the previous week looking over the campus they fully expected would be their home
come the fall. By late afternoon they had rented the front
room of a private home that was situated close to the bustling
downtown section.

Shortly afterwards George called on Joe Swetish, now
operating the popular Bijou Smoke Shop on the corner of
Brush Alley and First Street, two doors away from the Bijou

Theatre. Swetish contacted friends at the Buick division of General Motors. The next morning Bahan and Gipp went to work for Buick Motors, Factory 12, Sheet Metal Division.

On the afternoon of June 16 Gipp and Bahan met with police commissioner Tex Morris, at which time Flint's most notorious cop signed them to a contract that bound them to play their baseball in the factory league as members of the Buick 12 team. George and his buddy thus joined the ranks of an illustrious list of itinerant ballplayers who had traveled to Flint that summer just to play baseball. Heading this list were such stars as Floyd Darland, Brute Shea, Bobby Curtiss, Joe Collins, Perry Ballmer, Dutch Brantigan, Red Coble, William Nicholls, Kid Kober, Mugs Milligan, and Harvey Sensenback, nearly all of whom played for the powerful Buick 38 entry. Like Buick 12, Buick 38 was a member of the Flint Factory League, one of the most popular of several automotive-sponsored leagues that were in operation during that summer. Unlike the popular semi-pro General Motors League, which played on Sundays, the Factory League was strictly amateur, each team playing twice weekly at the twilight hour.

Begun in 1919, the Factory League was but a part of an extensive recreational program sponsored by the car makers for the enjoyment of their vast legion of employees. In a running competition with other industrial cities such as Detroit, Cleveland, Akron, and Cincinnati, which maintained interfactory sports programs the year round, Flint auto builders sponsored such in-season sports as football, basketball, and hockey. Aware of the need for a program that encouraged family events, the companies provided the facilities for such affairs as company picnics and cotillions, the music for the latter being supplied by orchestras formed from within individual factories. From the outset, however, it was apparent that of all the company-sponsored activities baseball was by far the most popular. With this in mind the Flint companies soon adopted the practice started in cities such as Kenosha, Wisconsin, by the Simmons Company and others, of recruiting exceptional athletes from all parts of the country, offering them jobs with the company for which they played. Pete Bahan best described this type of job when he stated, "Little more was required of George and me at Buick 12 other than to report for work each day."

This recruitment practice went into operation on a grand scale in 1920, and its effects became immediately apparent to the baseball public. Sportswriter Tip O'Neill, for one, attributed the large turnout at the games played at Athletic Park to what he said was "a better brand of baseball than in previous years."

By the time Gipp got to Flint the baseball season was already in full swing, and Buick 38 had already begun to project its dominance over the rest of the league. Unbeaten in its first ten games, this powerful nine looked as if it had come straight out of a fast-paced professional league—and for good reason. Some of its players, such as Kid Kober and Mugs Milligan, were ex-big leaguers, while the rest of its starters had seen service in either the Northern Canada League or the Michigan-Ontario League, commonly referred to in the area as the Mint League.

Complementing this group of former professionals were three of the best pitchers in the league: Bobby Curtiss, Perry Ballmer, and Steve McKan. The kingpin of the trio was Curtiss, a tall, lean southpaw who once pitched for his home-town Toledo Rail Lights, a well-known independent semi-pro team that numbered among its victims many of the best major league teams of both the National and American Leagues. While hurling for the Rail Lights, Curtiss was spotted by a scout and given a contract with the Chicago White Sox. His major league career was cut short after only one season, however, when, while teaching carpentry at

Waite High School in Toledo during the off-season, he amputated several fingers of his pitching hand in a freak shop accident.

While at Waite, Curtiss, who doubled as baseball coach, discovered Perry Ballmer, then a student at the school. A natural athlete, Ballmer was a star performer on the school's great basketball team and, after several weeks of working with Curtiss in the spring, went on to become one of the best high school pitchers in the state. In his senior year he joined an independent ball club in Toledo and went on to win twenty-three straight games, whereupon Connie Mack offered him a three-year contract with the Philadelphia Athletics. Ballmer turned it down, however, because his mother wanted him to finish high school. After graduation Ballmer played professional baseball briefly with London of the Mint League. He was still on their roster in the spring of 1920 when he and Bobby Curtiss met with Archie Campbell, the athletically minded boy genius of the automotive world, who on behalf of General Motors signed the pair to a contract to play baseball in the Flint Factory League.

Of the pair Ballmer was the more popular with fans, both on and off the field. He was to share his popularity not only with George Gipp but also with a young man named Hazen Shirley "Kiki" Cuyler who played left field for Buick 1. Born in the small mining town of Harrisville, Michigan, Cuyler was one of those splendidly conditioned athletes who never drank or smoked and who possessed all the desire needed to reach the top. Standing five-feet-eleven and tipping the scales at 185-pounds, Cuyler, like Gipp, batted and threw right-handed. He also had a fine throwing arm and ran the bases with speed and daring. Cuyler had come to Flint for two reasons: to get a little experience playing against pros, and to be seen by major league scouts. Flint was to provide him with both these opportunities.

Another similarity shared by Cuyler and Gipp was that

both played on losing teams that summer. The Buick 12 team turned out to be the only team on which George ever played to finish its season with a losing record—Buick 12 ended up with an eleven win, twelve loss mark.

That Buick 12 finished a game below the .500 mark was no reflection on Gipp. As he was to prove the first time he put on a uniform, Gipp had come to Flint to play baseball. In his first game, playing against Buick 11 (which boasted the city's biggest shop), he cracked out two hits on three official times at bat; his second hit, a double, drove in runners from second and third. After that there was no stopping the irrepressible Gipp. In less than two weeks he was hitting well over .300 and was closing in on the league leaders in both runs scored and home runs. Defensively, he was hauling in drives that only someone with preternatural abilities had a chance to catch. And when he wasn't robbing batters of base hits, he was throwing them out on the base paths with an arm that was as deadly and accurate as a Springfield rifle. In a game against Buick 11 George raced back to deepest center field, caught a ball that had caromed off the top of the Lakeside roller coaster, and threw the batter out at second base.

With one electrifying performance after another to his credit, the great Notre Dame star began to draw the attention of teams in the General Motors Industrial League. Buick 38 manager Archie Hickman offered George fifty dollars a game if he'd consent to play for them on Sundays. Determined to maintain his amateur status, George declined. Finally, however, after much personal deliberation, George consented to play for Dort Motors with the stipulation that no money would change hands.

Playing with Dort, George became acquainted with Joe Collard and Emery Hehn, two exciting players who had come to Flint mainly to work at General Motors. Collard, a versatile ballplayer from Reed City, was a fine batsman who turned out to be a winning pitcher also, posting a 7-0 mark in the Factory League that season. Now retired and president of Flint's Old-Timers Baseball Association, the one-time terror of the Factory League recalls both Cuyler and his former teammate, Gipp.

"Cuyler could do it all—speed, hitting, excellent throwing arm. He used to come often during those days in Flint and ask me if I thought he could make it. I used to tell him with his talent the only place was up."

Collard, who pitched for and managed Durand, a semi-pro team, and had occasion to hire Detroit's great Hall of Famer Charley Gehringer for $7.50 a game, was as impressed with George as he was with the youthful Cuyler.

"George was a most likable fellow, always smiling, very good-natured and humorous. He was a fine outfielder and an excellent base runner. He was very deceptive in his movements, giving you the impression of not trying, but he had such fine coordination that he always seemed to do the job, getting under fly balls or stealing a base with nothing to spare. He always seemed to know just how much effort was needed for the situation. I hear tell it was the same when he played football."

Like all those who came into contact with George for any length of time, Collard was impressed by Gipp's smoking habits. "He always had a butt in his mouth, and one day I mentioned this to him and he said, 'Every time I go back to Notre Dame I say I'm going to quit smoking, and I end up smoking more than ever.'"

Shortly after Gipp became a Sunday teammate of Collard's on Dort-Lakeside, he received an urgent telegram from pool room owner Jimmy O'Brien back at Calumet. O'Brien, a staunch Notre Dame supporter, had succeeded Swetish as the manager of the Calumet baseball team, which was having a difficult time in quest of a second straight championship. Scheduled to play powerful Hancock on July 11, O'Brien asked Gipp to make it home and help insure a Calumet victory. Apparently still loyal to his pals back home, George consented, took the train up from Flint, and backed up the four-hit pitching of Paul Hogan with a single, a triple, and three RBIs in the 5-0 winning effort. A week later he came home once more to lead Calumet to a 2-0 victory over Houghton, keeping Calumet in contention for the league title.

In the ninth inning of the Houghton game, as George got ready to step up to the plate in what would be his last base-ball appearance in his hometown, Joe Savinni, who batted behind him in the order, asked George how he felt he would do in football at Notre Dame come fall.

"I'm really going to show them something this year," George replied, in what must rank as one of the most remark-able sports prophecies of all time.

Upon his return to Flint George took right up where he had left off, playing two days a week with Buick 12 in the Factory League and spending his Sundays in the outfield of the Dort-Lakeside nine. On one Sunday in early August, however, when Dort found itself with an open date, George accompanied a pick-up team to Rochester, Michigan, for a double-header with the town's highly acclaimed semi-pro nine. Gipp, who played shortstop in one of the games, was the hero of one of the two wins recorded by the Flint nine that day, smacking a home run off Ralph Wesley Judd, the strong-armed Ohioan who went on to pitch for two seasons with the New York Giants.

Three days after he hit his tremendous home run off Judd, George was back in center field for the Buick 12 team as they went up against Buick 1 and Kiki Cuyler. This contest, played on August 10, marked the only time that year that local fans were afforded the opportunity to see both these great stars in action at the same time. Shortly after the contest Cuyler, who the day before had signed with Bay City of the Mint League, left town to join his new team. In this particular contest Cuyler, who had been hitting at a .380 clip, was able to get only one hit in four at-bats off Parton, who scattered eight hits in posting a 3-2 win.*

Gipp, who had no plans to go anywhere that night, emerged from the contest as the undisputed star. He collected two hits in three official trips to the plate. The first was a triple, the second, a screeching ground single that was hit so hard it spun Buick 1's second baseman completely around trying to snare it.

The next day the *Flint Journal* spared no superlatives in its praise of Gipp, whom sportswriter Harry Dayton called the most exciting baseball player ever to come to Flint. Of interest, too, was the brief mention of two pregame stunts put on by Gipp, the first performed solo, the second involving teammate Bud Slomar.

In his solo performance Gipp enthralled the large crowd on hand with an uncanny display of drop kicking, as he booted several footballs over the left field fence. In the second stunt Gipp drew a tremendous howl from the fans as he threw a baseball with all of his force at the head of the hatless Slomar, who did not so much as blink as the ball caromed off the side of his head. To appreciate this trick that, at first glance, might seem more brutal than entertaining, one must first understand the victim.

Slomar, a star football and basketball player at the University of Kentucky the previous winter, was one of those wacky characters who seem to step right out of the pages of one of William Saroyan's early short stories. Besides being a ver-

---

*After a brief stay with Bay City, Cuyler went on to the major leagues, where he capped a long and illustrious career with a lifetime batting mark of .321. In 1968 he was elected to baseball's Hall of Fame.

satile athlete, Slomar was a fine musician who played a mean saxophone with the Buick 12 orchestra. He first came to the notice of the Flint sporting set when he outpointed Guy Buckles in a boxing match that was the main feature of Buick's camp show. Slomar's greatest claim to fame, however, came from his unusual physical stamina and strength. He was able to stay in water, swimming and floating, for as long as five hours, and he could stay underwater for five full minutes with little or no difficulty. He dared any man his own weight to try to knock him to the ground from a punch thrown squarely at his jaw. He was proudest of all, however, of what seems to have been a concrete cranium. Claiming that he'd suffer no ill effects from a baseball thrown at his head, he imposed upon Gipp, recognized as one of the strongest arms in Flint, to help prove his claim. Gipp reluctantly obliged, and the stunt became a ritual before each game. Commenting on the stunt, Gipp once told sportswriter Harry Dayton, "I mustn't have much of an arm if someone can catch one of my throws with his head."

Between his pregame stunts and his spectacular diamond exploits, George rapidly created an impression on the local sports scene that was destined to outlast him by more than a half-century. His diamond deeds, however, seem at times to pale by comparison to the reputation he built for himself off the field. Everywhere he went in town he was greeted and treated in a manner reserved for people of distinction. Merchants went to extremes to please him; waitresses fussed over him like a mother over a favorite son; and kids who caught a glimpse of him on the street rushed to his side just to be close. At the Elks Club and several local billiards parlors George's easy manner, good nature, and strong masculine proclivities made him a resounding hit with the menfolk, while his good looks and a bearing that a friend once described as "magnificent and unforgettable" had another effect entirely on the distaff side. Archie Campbell, for one, recalls that "a lot of pretty young ladies were chasing after him during that summer in Flint."

According to Pete Bahan, an extremely handsome fellow in his own right who combed his hair in the slicked-down fashion affected by the screen idols of the day, he and George double-dated frequently while in Flint. On occasion, when time permitted it, they even traveled to Detroit to see a number of young ladies they had met on their earlier trip to that city.

One of the favorite public spots of young couples in Flint at this time was the giant Lakeside Amusement Park on Peer Avenue. There on any given Sunday famous acts such as the Six Flying LaVans could be seen for the admission price of ten cents. Aside from such breathtaking performers, what made the park appealing to young lovers was its magnificent dance pavillion, which featured a dance contest held twice a week for six weeks during the height of the summer season. While attending one such dance, Gipp decided to enter the elimination contest.

As a partner he chose an attractive, unescorted young lady from the large group of young women rimming the dance floor. George and his partner, dancing the waltz and the fox trot, put on two spectacular demonstrations and were acclaimed the winners by the judges. For her effort the young lady received a diamond ring, and George was awarded a gold wrist watch.

If Flint friends such as Joe Collard had occasion to notice George's extremely large feet as he danced, others had much more opportunity to notice his outsized hands, especially when somebody gave him the "makings" and he showed off just a little by rolling a cigarette with one hand. Sometimes while visiting the local Elks Club George would give a demonstration of tricky card shuffling, including an adroit exercise in dealing from the bottom.

To the many Flintites who still have vivid recollections of

George Gipp, he appears to have been a carefree, happy-go-lucky man who hadn't a care in the world. Quite the contrary, however, for soon after he arrived in Flint George began writing to Iris regularly, and in return for a half-dozen letters he received only one hastily written postcard. Dismayed by Iris's reluctance to answer his letters, George arranged for a brief leave of absence from his job, and in early August he went down to Indianapolis to see her. Four days later he returned to Flint, at which time he told roommate Pete Bahan that everything was all right between them and he had never been happier in his life. Furthermore, after talking things over with Iris on the mezzanine of the Claypool Hotel, he had decided to renege on his agreement to attend the University of Detroit that fall and planned instead to return to Notre Dame, where he promised Iris he would work hard to get his degree. She, in turn, gave her promise to marry him.

Three weeks after Gipp's return from Indianapolis the Factory League's season came to an end, but not before Gipp, in his last game against Chevrolet, managed to collect three hits, a double and two singles, in four times at bat. George also finished the last three innings of the game on the mound for the losers. Even so, his feat seems to have been anticlimactic. Only the day before league president Frank Kelly had announced that the powerful Buick 38 team, after compiling a remarkable record of twenty-five wins and no defeats, would be awarded the pennant.

Two days after the close of the Factory League season Gipp was back playing for Dort-Lakeside. Their opponent was Buick 38, now a sure bet to capture the General Motors League title also. On the mound for Buick 38 that Sunday afternoon was their unbeaten ace, Perry Ballmer, whose string of fifty-one scoreless innings included five straight shut-outs. Led by Gipp, the Dort team pulled off the upset of the season, knocking off Ballmer and Buick 38, 9-8 in a ten-inning affair.

An interesting sidelight to this game occurred afterward when Gipp and Emery Hehn, the Dort catcher, went back to the clubroom to shower and change into street clothes. As they sat on the bench getting undressed, George suddenly jumped up and shouted, "Hey! I left $600 in my pants." When he checked them, hanging on a wall peg, he discovered to his relief that the wallet and money were still there.

Gipp's fine performance against Ballmer and Buick 38 marked a fitting climax to what had been a brilliant summer of baseball for him. In 14 games played that summer—10 with Buick 12 and the other 4 with Dort-Lakeside—he stole 6 bases and hit at a .375 clip, with 18 hits in 48 trips to the plate. Included in these 18 hits were 3 doubles, 3 triples, and 3 home runs. Defensively, he fielded an incredible .964, with 19 put-outs, 8 assists, and only 1 error. The error came not in the outfield but during a brief stint at shortstop during one of the games. Although George's brilliant hitting and fielding is still a source of conversation among old-time Flint baseball fans, what is remembered most is two of the three home runs he hit while there. One homer cleared the scoreboard at Athletic Park; the other sailed high over the gigantic roller coaster at Lakeside Amusement Park. These two drives are said by many to be the longest ever hit in Flint baseball history.

With the Dort-Lakeside victory over Buick 38, the regular baseball season in Flint came to an end. Nevertheless, Gipp still managed to provide newsmen with good copy. For example, the August 20 edition of the *Flint Journal* carried the following piece on its sports page:

We are pleased to report that George Gipp plans to play with Dort-Lakeside on Sunday against the Saginaw semi-pros.

Gipp, the Notre Dame star who makes all the uniforms look small, showed the patrons of last Sunday that he has the Gimp and will be a big attraction, particularly with Copper Country fans. The Calumet-Laurium club, which he was with last year, wired him to come for a tie-breaking game with Keweenaw come next Sunday, but he turned the offer down.

Several interests have approached Gipp about playing football this fall. Being of the Notre Dame club, he will probably return to college about September 25. He is, however, wavering whether or not he will drop his law courses for industrial pursuits.

Flint [which at the time planned to start a pro team] has a good chance at gaining his gridiron services as has Jim Thorpe, who offered him several hundred dollars a game both last summer and this.°

None of the possibilities mentioned in the *Journal* article came to pass. What's more, instead of the predicted date of September 25, George left town on September 5, boarding a train that took him to Calumet after a brief lay-over in Chicago. During this lay-over, George, while walking along one of the Loop's busy streets, accidentally ran into Ojay Larson.

"It was early evening," Larson said, "and as he had not eaten his dinner he invited me into a restaurant for dessert and coffee while he had something to eat. While we talked, he told me he was on his way back from Flint and was scheduled to take the next train to Calumet. At that moment he was still undecided on whether to complete his trip to Calumet or change his ticket for one to Indianapolis. He informed me that he had met a young lady with whom he was enamoured and that she was a strong factor in his dilemma.

°Thorpe was the owner and star of Canton, a powerful professional team.

He said it was now costing him about sixty-five dollars a month to call her long distance. Anyway, he said, if he did decide finally to go to Calumet, it would be his last visit there."

After bidding Larson farewell, George went back to the train depot and, instead of changing his ticket, waited for the train that would take him to Calumet. He spent about twenty-four days at home visiting with family and friends. The visit was capped by his stunning victory over an itinerant pool shark who traveled with a carnival that happened to be in Calumet at the time.

On his last day home George, accompanied by his friend Alger Train, visited the office of Dr. A. C. Roche, who advised him to have his chronically infected tonsils removed before leaving for South Bend.

On the way home Gipp said that he definitely would not have them taken out, admitting to Alger that he was more than a little afraid of "the knife." Several hours later Gipp took his seat on a train that rumbled out of the Calumet station bound for South Bend, Indiana.

13.

Gipp's Aerials Bomb Army

George Gipp arrived at South Bend on Wednesday, September 29, to begin his fourth and final year at Notre Dame.

The first thing he did upon arriving was to check into Sorin Hall, at which time he chose the only small room in the basement quarters—a choice, it seems, he made mainly to avoid having roommates. Later in the afternoon he walked over to the Registrar's Office and signed up for his courses: commercial law actions, personal property, contracts, elements of law, and torts.

On Friday afternoon George showed up at Cartier Field in time to run through a signal drill that Rockne and his new assistant, Walter Halas, had scheduled. Shortly afterwards, a pleased Knute Rockne met the *Tribune's* Arch Ward and pronounced his team fit for battle next day. Despite his tardiness, George Gipp would start at his familiar left halfback position.

154

On October 2 the Fighting Irish kicked off to Kalamazoo at 3:30 P.M. before five thousand fans, the largest crowd yet to see a season's opener at South Bend. George Gipp was in the starting line-up. Clearing his way were Roger Kiley and Eddie Anderson at ends, Hunk Anderson and Clipper Smith at guards, Frank Coughlin and Buck Shaw at tackles, and Ojay Larson at center. Joe Brandy was the quarterback, with Norm Barry at right halfback and Chet "Chetter" Wynne in the fullback slot.

Rockne's second team, with Carberry and Hayes at ends, Garvey and Moss at tackles, Dooley and Degree at guards, Mehre at center, Grant at quarterback, Mohardt and Danny Coughlin at halfbacks, and Castner at fullback, was to see plenty of action before the season was over. Considered by many to be good enough to represent any college in the country, this second unit offered Rockne a chance to experiment with the idea of starting his second team in games; he could wear down the opposition and make them easy prey for a fresh first team that would storm onto the field to start the second quarter. Known as the shock troops, Rockne's second unit would, after 1921, start many of the Notre Dame games, and it has been said that just seeing eleven new men rush onto the field was enough to demoralize many of Notre Dame's opponents.

From the outset it looked as if the Kalamazoo contest called for Rockne's spirited second unit. After only two minutes of play the Fighting Irish, showing no respect for the boys from Celery City, chalked up the first of many touchdowns. Two minutes later, Gipp, cutting through the line on play 51 with the precision of a lapidary, scampered to the Kazoo 20. Gipp and Barry then combined to carry the ball to the 8; two plays later Gipp hit off tackle for 5 yards and a touchdown. From there the Irish went on to win in a romp, 39-0.

A little-known incident that occurred in the Kalamazoo game was recalled by Roger Kiley, the superb pass-catching left end who came on strong in fall practice to nail down the post vacated by Bernie Kirk. The story lends itself well to pointing up the patience and understanding Gipp could show to an errant teammate.

Kiley, playing in his first varsity game that afternoon, was hampered by a bad case of the jitters. In the opening moments Gipp spotted Kiley wide open down field and hit him with a perfectly thrown pass. Kiley let it drop to the ground. "If a gate had been open I would have run to Chicago," Kiley said. "There was no way out, and I came back to the huddle. George said to Brandy, 'Joe, call it again.' Joe did. I caught the next pass and several others. After the game George said to me, 'Roge, come out fifteen minutes early next week and we'll get better acquainted, and we'll stand them on their heads.'"

The next Saturday thirty-five hundred fans turned out at Cartier Field for the team's encounter with Western State Normal. In a contest marred by heavy penalties and extreme heat, the Rockne men showed their loyal followers that their easy victory the week before had by no means been a fluke. They battered the heavier Normalites into submission by a score of 41-0.

While a rugged Notre Dame defense dropped the Normalite backs for repeated losses, Gipp led a devastating Irish ground attack. Even though two of his touchdown jaunts were called back because of penalties, he still managed to pile up 123 yards on the ground in only fourteen rushes, while completing one of two passes for an additional 10 yards.

One week later Notre Dame traveled to Lincoln to oppose Henry Schulte's powerful Cornhuskers of Nebraska. Paced by an awesome front wall that consisted of Swanson and Scherer at ends, Pucelik and Welles at tackles, W. Munn

and M. Munn at guards, and Day at center, the Cornhuskers
were coming into the contest as the favorites, picked by
sportswriters as a three-point choice to win the second
rubber match of a series that had begun six years before.
(Both teams had two victories apiece, with the 1918 contest
ending in a scoreless tie.)

The Irish tried to get things going early with a surprise
play. On a first-and-ten on his own 20, Gipp, on the first
play of the game from scrimmage, dropped back to his
own 15 and uncorked a long pass that halfback Norm
Barry, standing alone at midfield, let slip through his fingers.
When the embarrassed Barry returned to the huddle, George
remarked cryptically, "Next time I'll put handle bars on it."

Buck Shaw got the Gold and Blue on the scoreboard
moments later, however, when he burst through the Cornhusker middle to nail Nebraska's Welles in the end zone for
a 2-point safety. Minutes later Nebraska drove to the Notre
Dame 4; Cornhusker Ernie Hubka went in for the touchdown on a wide end sweep, after which Day's kick made it
7-2 Nebraska.

After two drives by the Irish failed to produce a much-
needed touchdown, a disgruntled Rockne had fullback
Bob Phelan warming up on the sidelines as the first quarter
came to an end. Paul Castner had started at the fullback
slot after Chet Wynne had come down with a bad case of
fumble-itis in the game the week before. During the time
out, Gipp approached Rockne.

"Rock—how about Chetter?"

"No," Rockne replied.

"Give him another chance," Gipp pleaded.

Reluctantly, Rockne consented.

On the first play of the second quarter Gipp, after a
beautiful block by Wynne, broke out into the clear and
raced 55 yards for a touchdown. The play was called back,

however, and Notre Dame players watched the referee walk off 15 yards against them. But Gipp was not to be denied— a series of passes, all of which he completed to right end Eddie Anderson, brought the ball to the Cornhusker 10. With first and goal to go, Wynne thrust up the middle for 8 yards; two plays later quarterback Brandy sneaked in for the score.

In the final quarter Chicagoan Norm Barry, the first player to come up through the minims and win a monogram, redeemed his first-quarter blunder by putting on a fine display of pass catching that helped the Irish put the game out of Nebraska's reach. A personal favorite of Gipp's on the playing field, Barry caught several of Gipp's passes, one of which put Notre Dame just inside the 20. Gipp, on a fake pass, powered himself up the middle, found some daylight, and galloped into the end zone for the Irish's last score of the game. Gipp led the Gold and Blue to a surprisingly easy 16-7 victory over the Cornhuskers; by his faith in his teammate Wynne, George also saved the young fullback's collegiate career. From that time on Wynne became Notre Dame's first-string fullback, a position he was to hold throughout his varsity playing days.

Nebraska's Leo Scherer, the right end who went on to win a berth on the All-Western eleven, said of Gipp, "I would call George one of the greatest. He was an outstanding back that day, and in those days we had a great defensive team. But still he made the necessary yardage. In the game the year before against us he made most of his yardage against Ray Lyman, the greatest defensive tackle Nebraska ever had—the same Lyman who later was an All-Pro tackle with the Chicago Bears."

Clarence Swanson, who played the other wing position for Nebraska and who went on to win All-American honors in 1921, said that Gipp, aside from giving Nebraska "fits," was

the best passer, runner, and kicker that he had ever seen.
What is even more interesting is Swanson's recollection of a
trick play used by the Irish in the 1920 game.

"Rockne dreamed up this fake play that was perfectly
legal," Swanson said. "The Notre Dame players advised
referee Quigley that at a certain time they would fake an injury but did not want time called out. They lined up with
seven men on the line; their center, Larson, however, feigned
an injury, dropped down, and lay on his stomach. Suddenly
he turned over and threw the ball back to Gipp, and he went
around us for a touchdown. We didn't even see him until he
got past us. Unfortunately for them, however, Johnny
Mohardt, who was the other halfback, was caught for clip-
ping, and the play was called back and Notre Dame was
penalized 15 yards. Gipp's words were, 'Don't mind, Johnny,
we'll soon have another one,' and it wasn't long before Mr.
Gipp came through with his promise."

After Nebraska the next team up on the Notre Dame
schedule was Valparaiso. But the Irish weren't concerned
about that game; they were thinking two weeks ahead, when
they would journey to West Point to meet mighty Army.

Arch Ward summed up the atmosphere in South Bend on
the morning of the Valparaiso game when he wrote the
following for his paper:

> If Notre Dame beats Valparaiso today, enthusiasm over the
> Army game will be rife next week. The Army has swept every-
> thing before it to date and is heralded as the strongest eleven
> that has represented the officers in a decade.
>
> Army scouts at Lincoln admitted they feared Notre Dame
> more than any team on their schedule. They said they will
> consider the season a glorious success if they triumph over
> Notre Dame, whatever be the outcome of the struggle with
> Navy.
>
> Reports emanating from Gotham state that many newspaper

experts will flock to the game in the hope of finding material for their mythical All-American eleven. For the first time since Notre Dame has invaded the East it is being recognized as a team of champion potentiality. Gipp, Brandy, Coughlin, H. Anderson, and Smith will be the cynosure of critical eyes when the two teams tangle on the wind-sprayed plains of the Hudson.

Meantime, the expectation of a sell-out crowd for the Notre Dame-Valparaiso game was realized when eight thousand fans jammed Cartier Field in time for the opening kick-off at 2:15 P.M., on Saturday, October 23. The crowd was somewhat disappointed when Rockne, playing a hunch, started his second unit, an unheard-of maneuver that, although it was to chagrin the Army scouts in the stands, was to do much for the growing reputation of Knute Rockne. The tactic demonstrated to the fans what those close to the Irish mentor had known for some time—that as an innovator Rockne was the archon of an order that was at least a quarter of a century ahead of its time. The second unit, playing a stout defensive game for a quarter and a half, made Rockne appear in the eyes of football pundits as a genius.

Although it was the Rockne innovation that drew the praise, it was the work of a trio of Upper Peninsula boys—Gipp, Anderson, and Larson, whom Rockne referred to as his "ski-jumpers."—that resulted in Notre Dame's pinning a 28-3 loss on Coach Koegan's Valparaiso eleven, a team that outweighed the Irish eight pounds to the man.

As Notre Dame prepared for its upcoming tilt against the vaunted Cadets, Knute Rockne made it a point to keep an eye on his great star. One of the methods he used to keep Gipp in line is recounted by John Brosnan, who came back to school too late that fall to qualify for a room on the campus. Forced to live in a downtown boarding house on St. Louis Boulevard, Brosnan, on those mornings when he rode the Hill Street trolley to the university, remembers seeing Gipp board the car downtown accompanied by Rockne, who was evidently there to make sure that George got to class.

Rockne is to be commended for keeping a close watch on Gipp, but one cannot help but wonder if it was necessary at this particular time. George, in keeping his promise to Iris, had settled himself down since returning to Notre Dame that fall. In fact he had become a good student, as we can see from a letter he wrote in October to his friend Paul Hogan in Calumet. In the letter George said that his engagement to Iris was on again, despite the strong objections of her father. George made it a point to mention that everything was fine at school and that his grades were up, for which he was happy. He concluded by informing Paul that for the first time in years everything was beginning to look up for him.

On Thursday, October 28, shortly before noon, Knute Rockne and twenty-three of his players boarded the New York Central train headed for West Point Military Academy, high on the west bank of the Hudson River some distance north of the stately skyscrapers of New York City.

Beneath a metallic grey sky and amid sporadic winds that cut through the heavy coats of the well-wishers lined up along the platform, the big train chugged out of the South Bend depot, accompanied by a gigantic roar from several thousand fans that was certain, as the Notre Dame fight song puts it, to "wake up the echoes cheering her name."

The long trip for the proud warriors from the little Midwestern school was movingly described by Hunk Anderson: "Notre Dame had allotted about $4,000 for the trip, so we had to go second class. We traveled by day coach; then that night we changed to Pullman. To cut down on expenses two guys were assigned to each of the lower and upper berths. Because of the high price of food on the train, we only had one full meal en route to the game, and for that we had to get off the train at Buffalo in order to find a cheap restaurant. Whenever any of the guys got hungry on the trip they'd jump off the train when it stopped, grab a quick bite, and be back before the train pulled out. None of us minded it though. We were just happy to go."

Led by the awesome backfield of Wilhide, Richards, Lawrence, and French, the Black Knights of the Hudson were coming into the conflict unbeaten and untied, having run over five previous foes with the gruesome finality of a fleet of tanks: Marshall College 40-0; Union 35-0; Middlebury 29-0; Springfield YMCA 27-7; and Tufts 27-6.

Army's quarterback, the wily Wilhide, was the man who engineered their accelerated offense to perfection, but their fleet fullback from New Jersey, Walter French, was the man responsible for making this attack the thing of perfection that it was. French, whose beautiful broken field running led most of the Army raids into enemy territory, could very well have been known as "The Magnificent Marauder from Moorestown." He was a swift and stylish runner who, like Gipp, could do everything well on a football field. He could pass, run, kick, and block with the best the game has ever produced, and like his Notre Dame counterpart, when the situation called for a field goal it was French who delivered. Standing five-feet-eight and weighing only 160 pounds, the agile French more than made up for his slight build with speed, skill, and quick thinking.

Before coming to West Point French had been a student at Rutgers University, where he became their first athlete to win three letters in one year: baseball, football, and basketball. The highlight of his days at Rutgers came at a class dinner, when members of a competing class kidnapped him and held him prisoner for two weeks. French escaped just in time to play on the school basketball team, which competed in the International Basketball Tournament at Atlanta,

Georgia. French led his team to a second-place finish. While at Rutgers he turned down a lucrative offer made by Connie Mack of the Philadelphia Athletics to play professional baseball.

At the Point French picked right up where he had left off at Rutgers, starring in baseball, basketball, and football. Before the start of the 1920 football season Eastern sports scribes picked French as an almost certain bet to win All-American honors.

Those familiar with French and Gipp saw the upcoming battle not so much as a clash between two unbeaten power-houses but rather as a match-up of two of the nation's finest backs. This aspect of the game engendered as much pregame excitement as the game itself and probably accounted for the heavy betting by students and fans alike.

With regard to one aspect of the betting, Hunk Anderson said, "We were approached by gamblers before we left for the Army game, but that wasn't unusual. Every time we went away to play they tried to get us to place bets for them. But we always refused to get mixed up in that kind of business. And by we, I mean George, also."

The night before the game Anderson, while relaxing in one of the barrack rooms provided by the Army, collected $2,100 from members of the Notre Dame team. Of that money $65 came from his own pocket, and $400 was handed to him by Gipp. The latter amount was soon to figure in a Gipp-Rockne clash that was to become legendary.

Later that same night Hunk met with the Army student manager, who assured Hunk that he could cover the amount. The next day, after the pair breakfasted together, they took the $4,200 to the local shoemaker's shop, run by an old man with a thick German accent. After placing the money in his safe, the cobbler turned to Hunk: "Are you coming back?"

"Don't worry," Hunk replied confidently, "I'll be back."

Later that afternoon ten thousand fans jammed into Army's stadium to witness the football game of the year. In this large crowd, which braved a stiff, icy breeze that swept across the West Point plains, were some of the most celebrated sports journalists of the day, including Grantland Rice, who had come up from New York City with the renowned Ring Lardner.

One of the first people the two writers encountered upon reaching the Point was Army Assistant Coach John J. McEwan, who Rice said later appeared to be "loaded with confidence." Lardner, whose love affair with Notre Dame was still as torrid as it had been in the days when he had been an anonymous South Bend sportswriter, looked McEwan directly in the eye and said, "I understand that Rockne is coming in again with that kid named Gipp."

"Who the hell is Gipp?" McEwan snorted.

"You'll find out at ten minutes to two tomorrow," Lardner replied.

McEwan did not have to wait until ten minutes to two before getting his first inkling of what Lardner meant. Some twenty-five minutes before the opening kick-off Gipp stunned McEwan and the partisan Army crowd by besting Cadet field goal expert Russell "Red" Reeder in an exciting pregame drop kick exhibition. From that point on the Army caissons were able to roll, but for the most part it was downhill.

Taking the opening kick-off, Notre Dame drove into Army territory only to have Chet Wynne fumble, whereupon Cadet right end Don Storck pounced on the ball on his own 37. Two plays later, Walter French skirted around left end for 40 yards, racing past Gipp, who made no attempt to stop him. On the next play, with the ball on the Irish 15, Lawrence smashed over the right side, saw daylight, and streaked into the end zone for the score. French's point after made it 7-0.

Gipp took the Army kick-off on his own goal line and galloped back to the 38 before being swarmed over by black-shirted Cadets. On a first-down play Gipp banged off tackle for 8; carrying the ball on the next play, he got enough for the first down, as well as a little something that was not expected. Emerging from the pile-up, Hunk Anderson began throwing punches wildly. Gipp rushed to his side. "What's the matter, Hunk?" Gipp asked.

"Some sonofabitch gave me the knee," Hunk roared.

Gipp tore off his helmet and was ready to mix it up with several of the Cadets nearest him when the referee rushed in between them. After restoring order, he walked off a 15-yard penalty against the Irish for unsportsmanlike conduct.

On the next play Gipp picked up the penalty yardage by racing around left end for 15 yards; two plays later he reeled off an additional 25 yards before being hauled down on the Army 29 in a great last-ditch tackle by French. Brandy fumbled on a sneak up the middle, but luckily he was able to recover the loose ball. On the following play Gipp dropped back to pass, spotted Roge Kiley wide open on the Cadet 5, and hit him with a perfectly thrown aerial. Johnny Mohardt slithered over right tackle for the score, and Gipp drop kicked the extra point to knot the count at 7 all.*

Early in the second quarter Gipp returned French's punt 57 yards before being brought down on the Army 38. On a first-and-ten Gipp faked a run, dropped back, and tossed a pass to Roge Kiley wide open on the 30. Running as swiftly as a cheetah on the hunt, Kiley outran the Cadet secondary

---

*In Gipp's time the player kicking the extra point had an option. He could take the ball out a minimum of 15 yards from the point where the ball had been carried over for the touchdown. Or, the kicker could stand on the 15 and boot the ball toward a receiver stationed on the goal line. Where the ball was caught marked the spot from which the point after would be attempted.

to give the Gold and Blue its second touchdown of the game. Once again Gipp drop kicked the point after.

Minutes later the formidable French took a Gipp punt and zig-zagged his way downfield 60 yards for a touchdown, after which the Cadet's one-man show booted the point after to tie up the game. Minutes later, as the clock indicated the approaching end of the half, French booted a field goal from 12 yards out. The Cadets went into their locker room at halftime leading 17-14.

A former Notre Dame star tells of an incident that occurred that vividly points up the conflicting attitudes of the great Notre Dame coach and his greatest star.

"Rockne, giving one of his finest halftime orations to date, was really putting it to the boys for being three points behind. He had just about finished when Gipp, standing nearby, asked for a drag on my cigarette. Rock loooked up and caught George leaning against the door, his helmet rakishly set atop his head, blowing out smoke. Rock's face turned purple. 'What about you, Gipp?' he snapped. 'I don't suppose you have any interest in this game?'

" 'Look, Rock,' Gipp replied, 'I got $400 bet on this game, and I'm not about to blow it.' "

As the third period got under way, Gipp, in a rare display of cockiness, told his teammates, "Look, you guys give me a little help and I'll beat this Army team."

On their first play from scrimmage Notre Dame, attempting to cross up the Cadets, tried a trick play that had worked perfectly some weeks before against Nebraska. Army's Don Storck describes it as well as its results:

On the preceding play Gipp had hit the middle of our line. As Notre Dame quickly lined up for the next play, George was slow in getting up, and the whole Notre Dame line relaxed, looking around at George. Ojay Larson, their center, was the only lineman to remain in position, bent over the ball. When quarterback Brandy called out to Gipp, "Are you all right, George?" the ball was snapped to Mohardt. We were waiting for it and came rushing through the relaxed Notre Dame line, throwing Mohardt for a big loss with George under the pile. As George got up he said to me, "Boy, we won't try that again —I could have been killed under there."

The third quarter, which featured some sterling defensive play, ended in a scoreless draw after Gipp, on a wide sweep around right end, pranced to the Cadet 20. On the first two plays of the final quarter Gipp, on two successive 5-yard bucks up the middle, got the Irish a first down on the Army 10. On the next play Brandy let Johnny Mohardt carry, and Notre Dame had its third touchdown of the game. Gipp's point after made it Notre Dame 21, Army 17.

After a series of downs brought the Cadets only 3 yards, French booted to the Notre Dame 7. Gipp gobbled it in and hauled it back to his own 45. On first-and-ten Gipp fired a pass to Roge Kiley, who snared it at the Army 34. Gipp came back on a tackle-eligible play to hit Frank Coughlin with a quick pass that was good for a first down on the Army 8-yard line. On the next play a fake criss-cross—Mohardt went to his right and Gipp to his left—allowed Chet Wynne to sneak up the middle unmolested for the score. Paul Castner booted the extra point that made it 28-17. And that was the last of the scoring for the day.

With less than three minutes remaining Rockne sent in Norm Barry to replace Gipp. What happened next is told by Roger Kiley:

"I have never seen an athlete get the acclamation he [Gipp] received when he walked off the field that day. He was tired and pale and his face was a little bloody, and the crowd at West Point stood up and nobody applauded. It was thrilling—awed silence."

With his brother Alexander in the stands cheering him on, George Gipp had put on one of the greatest performances of his career. Gipp's statistics were as follows: 150 yards gained in twenty rushes; 123 yards picked up as a result of five completed passes out of nine attempts; an additional 112 yards gained in running back punts and kick-offs. All of this was against one of the greatest teams of the era.

Despite Gipp's brilliant performance on the field, one of the most memorable moments of the afternoon occurred shortly after George left the field and took a seat on the Notre Dame bench to watch the final minutes of action. To those critics of George who have accused him of being self-centered, lacking in school loyalty, and indifferent to his team's fortunes, Father Charles L. O'Donnell, who happened to be seated on the Irish bench, has left behind a moving description of what he witnessed:

"He had done everything that any football player had ever done upon a field, and he had done it better than most. Darkness was coming in on the bitter winds that swept across the plains as he sat there in his blanket, relaxed, pale, silent, crying a little, I think. Then suddenly he was on his feet. He leaped onto the bench; the blanket had fallen from his shoulders.

"Chet Wynne, our fullback, had made one of his amazing cuts through the line, good for some fifteen or twenty yards. In a voice that could be heard, it seemed to me, above all the roar of the crowd, Gipp shouted: 'Yea, Chet!' as he stood there, self entirely forgotten, quivering from head to toe with joy and loyal pride in the achievement of a teammate."

Outside, some hours after the game, Grantland Rice bumped into a dejected John McEwan.

"How'd you like Gipp as a football player?" asked Rice.

"Gipp is no football player," McEwan snapped. "He's a runaway sonofabitch."

The next day the press was full of accounts of George Gipp.

CHICAGO JOURNAL

George Gipp, whose playing was the sensation of the West Point-Notre Dame game Saturday, is being proclaimed the greatest football man of the year. It is believed that his work in the game with the Army has cinched him a place on the All-American team this year.

CHICAGO HERALD

George Gipp of Notre Dame is heralded as the wonder man of football in New York today. Not since the days of Ted Coy of Yale has the East seen such a brilliant gridiron performance as Gipp put on at West Point yesterday. Every New York newspaper declares Gipp is All-American timber. Notre Dame had two teams on the field, said one paper—George Gipp and ten other men.

CHICAGO AMERICAN

Gipp was taken out of the game just before the close to save him for the Purdue contest Saturday. The Cadets gazed at the wonder man with sorrow and admiration as he staggered off the field.

NEW YORK TIMES

Gipp is a tireless worker and was as irrepressible a citizen as ever decorated an Eastern gridiron.

INTERNATIONAL NEWS SERVICE

George Gipp against the soldiers gave the rooters thrills galore, and critics pronounced him the greatest halfback ever seen on an Eastern gridiron.

NEW YORK HERALD

George Gipp is All-American or there are no real All-Americans this season. If anything can be done on a football field which Gipp didn't do yesterday, it is not discernible to the naked eye.

Army's great star, Walter French, while impressed with

the tight fit of the Notre Dame uniforms, had nothing but admiration for Gipp. French said of Gipp, "He was fantastic at all times, especially in the fourth quarter."*

Two other Cadets who had great praise for Gipp's performance were W. Fritz Breidster and Donald G. Storck. Said Breidster, "Gipp just would not be stopped." Storck had this to say: "Whatever he did, it was done with apparently little effort but with grace and agility. His long-legged, elusive gallops through our defense on that day in late October were as difficult to stop as might be those of an antelope in an open field. His long strides made his deceptive speed difficult to time, with the result that most of the time we were tackling thin air."

Army's Francis M. Greene made what was perhaps the most poignant observation of all regarding Gipp, and it had nothing to do with his performance that day. "Several of us saw Gipp in the shower room after the game and were shocked to see how emaciated he was. He was literally down to skin and bones, and it was much discussed in the squad room later."

---

*Another Notre Dame player who impressed French was halfback Johnny Mohardt. According to French, Mohardt was not far behind Gipp and may have been a shade faster. French and Mohardt, who were about the same size, traded clothes that Saturday night in New York's Astor Hotel at a banquet for the Notre Dame team hosted by the West Point alumni. French said John looked good in a West Point uniform, but his hair, a bit too long, gave him away.

14.

Short-lived Glory

A jubilant Notre Dame team, somewhat exhausted after a night out in the big town, left New York early Sunday morning. Although it was well after midnight when the train pulled into the South Bend station, a large, noisy crowd was on hand to welcome home the conquering heroes.

As the cheering crowd converged on the train, a modest George Gipp, wishing to avoid the idolatrous onslaught, quickly made his way through several of the adjoining cars. Before alighting from a coach near the end of the platform, George caught a glimpse of Bonnie Rockne standing well back from the crowd. In her arms she cradled her youngest child. George walked over to where she stood, relieved her of the baby, and together they watched the joyous festivities, which included a brief, spontaneous statement made by Bonnie's husband in his usual staccato style.

171

Five days later on the eve of the big game against Purdue, the Gipp modesty was still very much in evidence, according to Arch Ward:

> The Notre Dame student body marched to the Oliver Hotel last night, where they serenaded the Purdue party in style approaching the queen's taste. After cheerleader Slaggert had strained his larynx with cheers for both teams, impromptu talks were given by Coach Scanlon, Captain Birk, Stanwood, Carmen, Wagner, and Murphy of the visiting squad. Cries for "Gipp, Gipp, All-American halfback" were rendered in vain, for Gipp as usual was nowhere to be found at the time for speech-making. Gipp limits his athletic activities to deeds on the gridiron.

The disappointment Gipp caused the fourteen hundred students disappeared the next day when Notre Dame took the field against the Boilermakers of Purdue. Playing in his last game on Cartier Field before an estimated twelve thousand spectators, one thousand of whom were alumni returning to South Bend to celebrate the school's first Homecoming Day, George put on a spectacular one-man show that was very nearly the equal of the one he had staged at West Point the week before.

In leading the Fighting Irish to a resounding 28-0 win, Gipp accumulated a grand total of 257 yards, 129 of which came from only ten totes of the pigskin. The remainder came from four completed aerials out of seven attempts. With old grad greats Frank Herring, Red Miller, Joe Sullivan, and Red Salmon looking on, George electrified the stands in the second period when, after a good block from Buck Shaw, he galloped 80 yards through the entire Boilermaker eleven for a touchdown.

Impressed by what he had seen, Red Salmon, best remembered by the Irish for his brilliant play at fullback during the 1902 season, paid George the ultimate tribute when he called him "the greatest ever to play for the old school."

Many of the Purdue players who absorbed the shock of the Fighting Irish's 28-0 whitewash still have vivid memories of Notre Dame's great left halfback. Ex-Army man William Swank, who played left guard, said, "One play I came across at an angle and caught him a few yards from the goal line. Just as I was tackling him, he dropped the ball, presumably a fumble, but it hit flat and bounced up just right for a teammate to pick it up and go on to the goal line. Not legal, but pretty smart, I'd say."

W. Lionel Claypool, the right tackle, said of Gipp, "If an all-time All-American team was selected, George Gipp would be on it."

Cecil Cooley, the Boilermakers' right guard, recalls his frustrating afternoon this way: "Gipp was most evasive— seemed to just step sideways at the right time or hop over me. Many times I was sure I had him, but most times ended up with empty hands. I can still remember very well looking around after he evaded me and see him going down the field weaving, sidestepping, hesitating, speeding up, and twisting like a young colt that had just got out through an open gate."

It seems appropriate at this time to pause and reflect momentarily on a common contention of recent years that those Notre Dame teams on which George Gipp starred were basically one-man teams and not the smooth-working, multi-talented elevens that were to represent the school in succeeding years. This contention was refuted by sportswriter Gene Kessler, who, though he couldn't possibly have envisioned such a latter-day allegation, made this observation after the Purdue game: "One of the biggest reasons the team wins is because these players work in harmony . . . . They have been taught by Rockne to play together, and Saturday illustrated what a smooth-running gridiron machine can do. Each man does his part, and the team works like the American Army did in France."

While ardent Notre Dame rooters pondered the vague possibility of a postseason clash with Eastern powerhouse Penn State, the Notre Dame football team, unbeaten in its last seventeen games, boarded a train at South Bend on Friday morning, November 12, en route to Indianapolis for what was expected to be a breather against the University of Indiana. So heavily favored were the Irish that South Bend gamblers found it difficult to place bets even after offering odds of ten to one. Even Gipp had trouble wagering a chunk of the sizable bank roll he brought with him to the City of Railroads. George spent most of Friday evening traipsing from one pool room to another trying to place bets on his team. What is interesting about his meanderings is the method he used. Concealing his identity, he would walk into a pool room and engage several of the patrons in a friendly conversation, after which he would inquire innocently about the odds on the upcoming game. Disappointed that nobody was interested in betting on the Hoosiers, he offered what he hoped would be the perfect inducement—his willingness to bet that a fellow on the Notre Dame team by the name of George Gipp would score more points than the Indiana team put together. On this proposition he was able to get only one small wager of $10.

Luckily, George had met John Welch, a resident of Indianapolis and an alumnus of Notre Dame, at the Oliver Hotel before the team had left for the game. Gipp gave Welch $100 to bet on the game; Welch was free to give any Hoosier bettor a fifteen-point spot.

On the morning of the game George had a more difficult

time trying to conceal his identity. For his column "Serving the Punch," which appeared in the *South Bend Tribune,* Gene Kessler wrote the following from his room at Indianapolis's Claypool Hotel:

> George Gipp walked up Illinois Street, and police thought it was an Indiana parade. George just can't evade the admirers. Someone wanted to know if Gipp took Eddie Welch along to fight off the crowds.*

Gipp, who got up early on the morning of the game, went over to the train depot to meet his sister Dolly, who had come from Kalamazoo to see her brother play. After getting Dolly registered at the Claypool, Gipp rode the elevator up to the hotel's mezzanine, where he was to meet Iris. This lovers' rendezvous was to deal George the first of several severe jolts he would receive before the long day came to an end. What happened on the mezzanine of the Claypool is described by a good friend, who met Gipp two weeks later at South Bend's Oliver Hotel:

"George was in low spirits, and he looked terrible. He said he met his girlfriend Iris at the Claypool Hotel before the Indiana game, and she had coldly informed him that she had married someone else. And George said the way she expressed it, he knew that she had been making a damned fool of him."

Meanwhile, on another floor of the Claypool, Gene Kessler was busy banging out the following comments on his trusty typewriter:

> The Claypool reminds us of the Oliver. It is buzzing with Notre Dame students. The distance to Washington Park isn't

---

*Kessler was referring to Jimmy Welch, co-owner of Jimmy and Goat's Place.

quite as far as the distance from Washington Street to Cartier Field, but the car service seems to be crudely handled, and most fans walk.

Apparently, Indianapolis sport fans were awfully fond of walking, for when the appointed 2:00 P.M. kick-off time arrived some fourteen thousand of them had crowded into Washington Park to see Notre Dame meet its toughest opponent of the season, by far the toughest George Gipp would come up against in his illustrious gridiron career.

Led by Charles "Chick" Mathys, who had come from that hotbed of professional football, Green Bay, to play for the Hoosiers, the underrated boys from Bloomington played one of the finest games of the season, one that would go down in the annals of Notre Dame football as one of the hardest ever fought by the Fighting Irish. All afternoon the little ex-soldier Mathys, who stood only five feet eight and weighed in at a mere 158 pounds, ripped holes in the vaunted Irish line. At the end of three periods the Hoosiers led 10-0. To the thousands of overconfident Irish fans who sat stunned in the bleachers, the upset of the season seemed to be in the making.

George Gipp, who according to Indianapolis writer Mary Bostwick "looked like an aviator in the leather jacket he wore before the start of the game," was standing on the sidelines next to Rockne. He had been there since early in the second quarter when, after being brought down on a vicious tackle by two hard-charging Hoosiers, he had sustained a severely separated left shoulder. As he stood there with a blanket draped over his cold and aching body, it looked to all, Rockne included, as if Notre Dame were on its way to losing its first game of the season, blowing its chances for a second straight Western title.

In South Bend scores of faithful followers gathered out

front of Hullie and Mike's to watch the progress of the game as it was relayed by Western Union and translated to the electric light bulbs of the Gridgraph. They let out a mighty roar as Gipp's replacement, Johnny Mohardt, broke away on a 25-yard gallop behind some beautiful blocking by Norm Barry. On the next play, Mohardt skirted around left end for 18 more yards, and the crowd in front of the cigar store went wild.

Back at Washington Park, Notre Dame rooters were on their feet for the first time applauding Mohardt, who had succeeded in putting the fight back into the Irish. From this point on Mohardt and Barry, rivals all season long for the right halfback spot, got the Gold and Blue ground game moving. Quarterback Brandy, using Mohardt and Barry on alternate plays, directed his attack at the vaunted Hoosier middle, and the pair pounded their way to the Indiana 1-yard line.

Two subsequent tries at the middle by each of them failed to gain, however, and at this moment the Notre Dame rooting section let out a thunderous ovation as George Gipp, his shoulder heavily taped, trotted back onto the field. Brandy's next call was 51 with Gipp carrying. George smashed over left tackle and was stopped cold. Brandy repeated the call, and this time George gave it everything he had, smashing over the goal line with such force that he almost sent the goal post tumbling to the ground. Amid the frenzy of Notre Dame rooters, Gipp converted the point after, and the Irish trailed by only three. But time was running out.

Gipp kicked off on the next play, and Minton brought it back to the Hoosier 30. George, who aided in the tackle, got up slowly, clutching his left shoulder. Mohardt went in to replace him. The Notre Dame line, looking like the line of old, stopped Mathys and company cold. In fact Indiana lost almost 5 yards in two rushes. With a third and 15, Eddie

Anderson broke through the defense and hit Cravens so hard that the ball popped out of his hands, and Chet Wynne fell on it at the 28.

Mohardt and Barry, still playing together like country cousins, slashed their way to the Hoosier 15. On the next play Gipp, back in for a slightly shaken Mohardt, dropped back, and everybody in the stands waited to see him attempt the drop kick that would tie the score. Instead the versatile George uncorked a pass to Eddie Anderson that was complete on the 1. On the next play, as the Hoosier forward wall drove in the direction of Gipp, Ojay Larson cut down Hoosier center Pierce with a textbook block and Joe Brandy smashed in for the score. Gipp missed the conversion, but at that point nobody cared. Notre Dame had come back to win 13-10.

The next day Mary Bostwick, understandably dismayed by the last-minute Irish victory, chose to ignore writing about the game in favor of some old-fashioned Midwestern raillery:

> While I think of it, why do they call them "The Irish"? The only real harp names on the regular team are Kiley and Coughlin. And what with two Americans and Larson, they might as well call them "The Swedes."

As for Gipp, she reported:

> George had two white ankle bands on over his blue stockings and was easily identified—otherwise he would not have been.

The come-from-behind Notre Dame victory was later described by Indiana's great backfield star Chick Mathys, who later went on to star for the Hammond team of the NFL:

"It is the one game in my football career of so long long ago that I have replayed over and over again in my memory, but it still comes out to a 13 - 10 defeat. We led the national champion of that year in every department of football; but a costly fumble recovered by Chet Wynne in the last moments of the game—our only fumble—lost it for us. We were proud of our great effort that day but were a sadly disappointed bunch of boys after the game."

Mathys, who won two cups for his play against the Irish— one for the longest run of the game (35 yards), the other for intercepting four passes—delivered an encomium on George Gipp that was as fitting as it was sincere:

"The Gipper was a legend in his own time, just like our Packer quarterback Bart Starr is in his, which is the greatest tribute that I could pay any athlete. His opponents feared him as he could do everything well—run, kick, and pass. He was a tall, handsome, friendly, All-American young man. His exploits on the gridiron are still talked about in this area because his home was about one hundred miles north of Green Bay, where good football players are not soon forgotten."

After the Indiana game George went back to the Claypool Hotel, where he had dinner with Knute Rockne. Later they were joined by Chick Mathys on the mezzanine, and the three had a long, friendly chat. Some time afterwards George left the Claypool and headed over to the Lincoln Hotel, where he met John Welch, who with his wife and two other couples was seated in one of the booths in the hotel coffee shop having doughnuts and coffee. The large circular clock high on the west wall indicated that it was 12:30. A.M., Sunday morning. George's left arm was in a sling, and even at a distance he looked extremely peaked.

Upon seeing George enter, Welch got up from his seat and walked over to the middle of the room to meet him. From his wallet Welch removed thirty-five dollars and handed them to George, explaining that he had given fifteen-point odds but, luckily for George, had only been able to place sixty-five dollars of the money.

In a rare display of affection George hugged him and said, "John, thanks. It's the first time I've smiled today."

Later in the morning, the Notre Dame team left Indianapolis. Instead of disembarking at South Bend with the rest of the boys, George continued on the train to Chicago, where he was to keep an appointment with his friend and former college teammate Grover Malone, now residing in the Windy City. Malone, who had taken over the coaching reins at Loyola Academy, had asked George to come down to give his players some pointers on the art of drop kicking. As it turned out, George, although tired and feeling much pain from his dislocated shoulder, spent three days in Chicago. What was even worse, on the day selected to teach the kids to drop kick a strong, icy wind blew across the field from Lake Michigan.

That same night Gipp, on the train back to South Bend, began to feel the first signs of a fresh cold coming on. The repercussions of that cold would rock a nation.

George confined himself to his bed at Sorin until the following Friday night, at which time he had a visitor in the person of Knute Rockne.

Rockne, who like Gipp had been plagued with bad tonsils since childhood, inquired about the health of his great star. After learning from George that it didn't seem to be too bad a cold, Rockne asked George how he felt about leaving that evening for Evanston, where the Irish would meet Northwestern the next day.

"Think you're up to the trip?" Rockne asked.

"I suppose so," George replied.

"If you're not feeling up to par when we get there, I don't intend using you," Rockne said.

"That's jake with me," George replied.

The Alumni Association, ignorant of George's poor physical condition, had designated that particular Saturday, November 20, as George Gipp Day. The proclamation was met enthusiastically by local fans, who filled almost thirty coaches of a train that left South Bend for Evanston on Saturday morning.

The game itself, which marked the renewal of a series that had been discontinued in 1903, was greatly overshadowed by the expected appearance on the gridiron of Notre Dame's potential All-American halfback, George Gipp. George Gipp Day had produced the largest crowd yet to see a Northwestern home game—twenty thousand fans.

A huge groan greeted the teams as they trotted out on the field and the crowd learned that John Mohardt and not George Gipp would start at left halfback for the Fighting Irish. Since neither the press nor the crowd had been told of George's illness, most of the fans took Rockne's reluctance to start Gipp at halfback as an affront to them as well as to the Northwestern football team. Consequently, through most of the game the fans remained irate, booing every conspicuous move made by the Notre Dame mentor along the sidelines. In between they chanted incessantly, "We want Gipp! We want Gipp!"

Finally, in the fourth quarter, with Notre Dame enjoying a comfortable lead, Rockne could ignore the chants no longer. He sent in Gipp even though he himself later said that Gipp was running a high fever. The field was ice-covered "with a wind off Lake Michigan that was cutting us all to the bone."

Though Rockne wanted George to make only a token appearance, Gipp performed as if his playing meant the difference between victory and defeat. With twenty thousand fans still up on their feet cheering wildly, George hit right end Eddie Anderson with a perfect pass that was good for

35 yards and a touchdown. Minutes later Gipp came back to hit Norm Barry with another aerial that traveled 55 yards through the air. Barry, pulling it in at the Wildcats' 15, raced unmolested into the end zone for the 6 points. The pass, which contributed to the Irish's 33-7 victory, was good for 70 yards and for many years stood as a Notre Dame record for a completed pass.

Commenting on this pass and others thrown by Gipp, Barry said, "With the smaller ball that's in use now, I feel sure George would have broken every pass record to date. He used to say, 'You be there, and the ball will be there.'"

In the final moments of the contest a tired George Gipp, visibly ill, gathered up what little energy remained in his ravaged body and tried to run back a Northwestern punt. In what has been described as one of the greatest examples of sportsmanship ever seen on a football field, the two Northwestern ends, downfield to cover the punt, met George at midfield and brought him down with the gentleness of a mother putting her sleeping baby into its crib.

After the game Gipp was met by his old friend Lyman Frimodig, who had come down from East Lansing to see the contest.

"I'll see you in East Lansing Thanksgiving Day, Frim," George said, referring to Notre Dame's upcoming game against Michigan A&M.

For recollections of this game by Notre Dame's opponents we turn to Stanley Hathaway and Northwestern's celebrated Penfield brothers, Graham and Henry.

Stanley Hathaway, who when he wasn't playing football was busy defending his 160-pound conference wrestling title, was notably impressed by Gipp's passing game. "When the ailing Gipp came in and tossed those two touchdown passes, that wrote *finis* to Northwestern's chances."

Team captain Graham Penfield, who got one of the guard berths on Walter Eckersall's Big Ten team, was also impressed by Gipp's passing, especially the low bomb that Anderson caught for a touchdown. "It was one of the best passes I've ever seen thrown."

Henry Penfield had the following comment: "When we came out for the second half, there was George warming up on the sidelines and throwing passes at least 50 yards. He went into the game later and, in spite of his illness, proved himself a very fine player and a real competitor. He was such an elusive runner and had such good blocking that I don't remember whether or not I ever got near enough to even try to tackle him."

In South Bend Notre Dame was awaiting word from Gene Kessler and Jack Kearns (Jack Dempsey's manager), who were in New Jersey trying to arrange a postseason game with Princeton. There was still no word from them when George Gipp returned with the team from Evanston. It was apparent to all who turned up at the station that George was a very sick young man. He had a bad case of chills, and later that night his temperature became dangerously high.

The seriousness of the illness was noted by Gipp himself, who after a brief visit to the home of George Hull showed up for an affair at the Oliver Hotel the following Monday night. The affair was the annual banquet of the South Bend Rotary Club, which had as its honored guests the Notre Dame football team.

Shortly before the speech-making, George confided in his buddy Hunk Anderson, "Hunk, I feel terrible. My throat's cutting me up, and I got a high fever."

"You better talk it over with Rock and maybe go to the hospital," Hunk replied.

A short time later Gipp called Rockne away from the seat he occupied at the speakers' table and confessed the severity of his illness. Rockne, who also felt that George belonged in the hospital, went ahead and made all the necessary arrangements.

15.

The Last Days

On Thanksgiving Day, November 25, Notre Dame closed out its second successive unbeaten, untied season by walking over Michigan A&M 25-0 before eight thousand disappointed fans at East Lansing. The fans' disappointment was caused by the absence of George Gipp from the Notre Dame line-up. Gipp, who was replaced by Johnny Mohardt, did not even make the trip with the team. He was confined to St. Joseph's Hospital in South Bend. A report emanating from the hospital the day before said that his condition was not serious, however, and it was expected that he would be released shortly.

George Gipp entered St. Joseph's Hospital early Tuesday morning, November 23, less than three hours after his conversation with Rockne at the Oliver Hotel. At the time of his admittance he complained of having a tender throat and chills. He was immediately put into a private room,

184

where one of the staff nurses took his temperature, which was near 104 degrees.

Shortly thereafter Doctor J. E. McMeel was called in to attend Gipp. After a preliminary examination Doctor Mc-Meel diagnosed Gipp's illness as tonsilitis. The diagnosis was shortly corroborated by Doctor Thomas Olney, a South Bend surgeon who shared offices with Dr. McMeel in town.

For the next several days George was confined to his bed, at which time aspirin was administered to him around the clock to relieve pain and reduce fever. At this time, also, a mixture of honey, borax, and glycerine was used twice daily to swab his tender throat. His diet was restricted to liquids.

After one week of this treatment Gipp's temperature had dropped several degrees, but his throat, which doctors had hoped would respond favorably to rest, proper diet, and aspirin, remained raw and severely painful. Unexpectedly, on November 30 the hospital issued a bulletin that George's condition suddenly had become critical. A hospital spokesman reported that George was now suffering from pneumonia, and that the next forty-eight hours would be critical.

Dr. McMeel met with several reporters outside the hospital and confirmed the bulletin. The doctor openly admitted that he was concerned about Gipp's condition and promised to do all that was medically possible.

By this time newspapers from New York to Los Angeles, aware of the seriousness of George's illness, had begun to publish daily reports on his condition, with the result that the eyes of an entire nation were focused on South Bend's St. Joseph's Hospital. Soon letters and telegrams from well-wishers all over the country began pouring into Notre Dame and the hospital.

In South Bend business had come to a standstill. Crowds gathered on street corners at all hours of the night and day, waiting, waiting for the next hospital bulletin. People who had never seen a football game stopped Knute Rockne on the street to inquire plaintively about the condition of Rockne's great star. Many of them further manifested their deep concern for Gipp by coming forth with offers to donate their blood if a transfusion became necessary. Night and day for the next week the hospital was besieged with phone calls from people who left their names in case blood was needed. Soon the list of names compiled by the hospital filled a dozen sheets of paper. All of these names were for a young man who found it difficult to remember someone's name, sometimes no matter how many times he had heard it.

Meanwhile, George lay in his hospital bed, his once-strong body ravaged by complications brought on by pneumonia. At this point his doctors decided to call in specialists for consultation. The next day Dr. T. O'Connor, an eye, ear, nose, and throat specialist, arrived from Chicago. Later that same day another noted Chicago physician, C. H. Johnson, followed O'Connor to South Bend.

These two physicians remained at Gipp's bedside for twenty-three consecutive hours, working fiercely to save his life. To bring down the high fever that was no longer responding to analgesics, Dover's powder was administered orally. The doctors also gave Gipp whiskey and intermittently applied ice packs to his forehead. Several enemas were given, plus a cough medicine to break up congestion. At one point digitalis was administered when the doctors became concerned that Gipp's heart was beginning to show signs of failing. Finally, shortly before noon on December 2, Gipp's fever broke, and his doctors announced joyfully that the great football star had won his bout with pneumonia. They were quick to warn, however, that the critical stage had not yet been passed, and though there was some room for optimism, the next few days were going to be crucial ones nevertheless. After a consultation later in the day, the doctors reported their consensus that Gipp would recover.

The next day the news hit the streets, and a nation breathed a deep sigh of relief. The Notre Dame students, now optimistic, nevertheless showed concern. The next morning the entire student body went to mass at Sacred Heart Church. Many of the students received communion for, as the editor of *The Dome* put it, "Big George."

Inside George's hospital room there was further rejoicing at his improved condition. His mother, his sister Dorothy, and his brother Matthew, all of whom had arrived in South Bend on November 29 and had remained at his bedside throughout the critical hours, were able to relax for the first time. George, although in a weakened condition, was proving himself to be in good spirits and, more encouragingly, was even able to carry on a conversation with members of his family.

As George had lain in his hospital bed surrounded by loved ones, the nation's sporting press had been busy with the business of selecting its All-American teams. In such cities as Philadelphia, Pittsburgh, Chicago, and New York, top sportswriters found a place for George Gipp on their All-American teams. On November 29, Neal O'Hara of the *Boston Post* became one of the first prominent Eastern writers to name George to a first-team berth. The next day Carl A. Reed, one of the best-known gridiron officials of the day, selected his team, which appeared in the *New York Herald* and was given quick endorsement by *Herald* football expert Daniels. Reed's choice for left halfback—George Gipp.

On November 30 the celebrated dean of football, Walter Camp, announced his All-American team in *Collier's Weekly*. On this, the most prestigious of all the teams announced, Camp named George Gipp as fullback on his first team. In naming George, Camp said:

> In the backfield Gipp of Notre Dame gets the first place on account of his versatility and power, able as he is to punt,

drop kick, forward pass, run, tackle—in fact do anything that any backfield man could ever be required to do and do it in well-nigh superlative fashion. He drop kicked on his freshman team 62 yards. When a man who has been taken off with a badly injured shoulder can go in on a pinch and carry the ball over the goal line to get his team an absolutely necessary touchdown, something of the man's power can well be understood.

Notification of Gipp's selection by Camp reached South Bend that same day, the day George's bout with pneumonia had reached its critical peak. The doctors conferred with Knute Rockne and decided that Gipp should be informed of his selection, in the hope that the news would give him a needed boost.

That afternoon Knute Rockne came to the hospital to see George. With him was his assistant, Walter Halas. With a broad smile across his face, Rockne bounced into the sick room and without bothering to acknowledge the presence of the other people in the room went straight to Gipp's bed. Bending over and speaking in a half-whisper, Rockne told George that Camp had selected him on his first team.

"How does that make you feel," Rockne asked, "knowing you're the first player in Notre Dame's history to receive the honor?"

Gipp smiled feebly. "Well, that's jake, Rock."

Even before the news of Camp's selection had time to register, Gipp received another bit of encouraging news. Chicago Cubs president Bill Veeck sent a wire to George reaffirming the lucrative baseball offer he had made several months before. In the wire Veeck mentioned that a new contract had been drawn up and was already in the mail.

The following day, big-league baseball great Johnny Evers stepped off the Twentieth Century Limited at Chicago's LaSalle Street station; one hour later Evers was named the new manager of the Chicago Cubs. Sometime later Evers met with the Chicago press, at which time he was asked what he thought of the possibility that Gipp might be playing for him.

Said Evers, "I admire his ability as a baseball player as well as a football player, and I know he'll qualify as a regular outfielder after a few weeks of training in the tropics."

Throughout the first week of December George's condition, as reported by hospital sources, remained about the same. He was still in serious condition, but that he had not suffered a relapse was viewed by his doctors as an optimistic sign, indicating that he might have passed the critical stage.

Hunk Anderson, who visited George daily at this time, noticed that George was in extremely high spirits, was able to navigate the room without help, and was even able to go to the bathroom down the hall without the aid of a nurse. This was corroborated by the son of George Hull, at whose home Gipp's mother had been staying since her arrival in South Bend. Stanley Hull recalls:

> My father worked a night on, night off shift at the cigar store. On the nights he worked I drove Mrs. Gipp to the hospital in my father's new car, a Studebaker Six. On the way there I'd stop off at the Rocknes' to pick up George's sister and brother who were staying with them. Between my father and me we made this trip for about two and a half weeks. I remember that George was very chipper and walked around the room a lot during visits, and they had a hard time keeping him in bed.

During that first week of December Gipp had two out-of-town friends come to visit him at the hospital. One was Iris, who came alone from Indianapolis and visited with him for about one hour. The other was Joe Swetish, who came by train from Flint.

On his return home Swetish, with tears streaming down his cheeks, recalled part of his visit with Gipp for *Journal* sportswriter Harry Dayton: "They wouldn't let me see the boy—but I got in. George said, 'What in hell you doing here?' I told him I heard he had been hurt playing football. I couldn't tell him the truth. But he knew. He told me, though, that he was better and would be out soon. He's still got 'em—guts—and I'm glad."

In between visits by family and friends, George supposedly began to show an interest in the Catholic religion. While he lay in his hospital bed he was apparently seeking answers concerning his soul, and one of the people who visited him frequently during this time was Father Pat Haggerty of Notre Dame. During one such visit, George, reportedly expressing his desire to become a Catholic, talked with Father Haggerty about conversion. As we shall see, the results of this visit were to engender a controversy between spokesmen for Notre Dame and relatives of Gipp that was destined to outlast George by half a century.

On Sunday, December 12, at eleven o'clock at night, it became apparent to George's doctors that the great athlete had suffered a relapse, and little hope was held by them at this time for his recovery. Miraculously, on Monday morning, George showed a slight improvement, but doctors were by this time hesitant to predict a recovery. Dr. McMeel said only that George was still in critical condition.

As Monday night drew on Gipp's condition again took a turn for the worse, and the young man who had been confined to his bed since Sunday began to show unmistakable signs of losing his fight for life. Around seven o'clock that night, December 13, his mother, who had been taken ill earlier in the day and had been forced by physicians to give up her twenty-four-hour bedside vigil, received a phone call at the Hull home. It was from the hospital, and they advised her to come at once.

At the time of the phone call, Father Pat Haggerty was making his fourth visit to Gipp's bedside that day. As had been the case in the priest's previous visits, when George saw him walk into the room he said, "Goodbye, father, goodbye, father." Although Father Haggerty obliged and left again, it should be noted here that the priest never fully understood just what Gipp meant when he uttered those words.

Outside, though night had fallen, it was still unseasonably warm for a December day in northern Indiana. At eight o'clock the temperature had reached a high of fifty-four degrees. The rain that had begun falling at daybreak was still coming down heavily as the Hulls' Studebaker Six, driven by Stanley and carrying George's mother, sister, and brother, pulled up at the front entrance to the hospital.

Except for Dr. McMeel and a nurse, George was alone when the four of them hurried into the room. Dr. McMeel looked at George's mother out of the corner of his eye and nodded his head slightly. Gipp, his face white as the pillow behind it, turned to pick himself up when he saw her. Knute Rockne, whose face was almost as ashen as Gipp's, came quietly into the room and stood behind the Gipps. At this point Stanley Hull, who was standing near the door, heard George cry out, "I'm not going to die—I'm going to play one more game for Rock."

At this time the nurse, realizing that Hull was not a member of the family, asked him to leave. Moments later Rockne, motioned forward by George, came up to the bedside and leaned over his great star. And it is said that at this time George whispered to Rockne:

"I've got to go, Rock. It's all right. I'm not afraid. Sometime, Rock, when the team's up against it, when things are wrong and the breaks are beating the boys—tell them to go in there with all they've got and win one for the Gipper. I don't know where I'll be then, Rock, but I'll know about it, and I'll be happy."

The surprising strength that George had displayed earlier slowly faded as the night wore on, and during the early morning hours it was apparent that he had grown much weaker. But still he remained conscious—this to the utter disbelief of his doctors, who stood in awe of what one termed his "unbelievable grit."

Shortly after two o'clock on that Tuesday, December 14, George looked up from his bed, smiled at his mother and sister, and then lapsed into a coma.

Moments later, with his mother, sister, and brother looking on, conditional baptism and conditional absolution were given George by Father Pat Haggerty. Afterwards a thin, bespectacled Father O'Hara administered extreme unction, the last rites of the Roman Catholic Church.*

Outside, the aura of a damp, rainy, miserable Midwestern night was almost a match for the immense gloom that pervaded the sickroom. In it a great athlete was fighting the greatest battle of his young life. A thousand miles to the east another great one, Jack Dempsey, was in quiet repose, preparing for his title defense that evening at Madison Square Garden against a contender by the name of Bill Brennan.

Downtown at the Oliver Hotel gambler friends of the dying football star also were waiting, waiting grimly for what seemed to be inevitable.

----

*Later Father Haggerty explained in a letter to a teammate of Gipp's that the conversion was one of interpreted intention as distinguished from concrete expression.

At 3:30 A.M. the final scene of the tragic drama unfolding at St. Joseph's Hospital was played, and minutes later a clerk at the Oliver flicked a switch that controlled all the lights in the hotel—a subtle signal that George Gipp was dead.

16.

Summing Up

THE drama that had played for three weeks at St. Joseph's Hospital had ended. The curtain had been brought down by what Gipp's doctors said had been streptococcal hemolytic septeropyemia, a fatal condition attributed to a severe infection of the throat. The infection could easily have been cleared up by the administration of penicillin, but the discovery of that wonder drug by Dr. Alexander Fleming was still almost a decade away.

With Gipp's death came the end of a nation's vigil. Those people who had waited anxiously each day for a medical report from St. Joseph's Hospital would wait no more. There would be no more reports. George Gipp was dead, and with his passing it seemed as if a mountain had come tumbling down before them. Many people were at a loss to explain it. Perhaps the editor of *The Dome* expressed it best when he wrote in gentle protest:

194

O Lady! You have taken of our best
To make a playmate for the Seraphim.
There on the wide sweet campus of the blest,
Be good to him.

Telegrams from all over the country poured into Notre
Dame following Gipp's death. They came from governors,
senators, congressmen, and the heads of colleges and universities. They came from other athletes, former athletes,
fans, and even people who cared nothing for sports. From
one end of the country to the other the death of George Gipp
had come as a hard blow.

Nowhere was the force of its impact more keenly felt than
in South Bend, the city that had grown first to love George
and later to adopt him as its own. For a while the heart of
this great Midwestern city had, like that of its most beloved
son, ceased to beat.

While Notre Dame's president, the Very Reverend James
A. Burns, was offering his deepest sympathy to the bereaved
mother of the great athlete, Knute Rockne, in a statement to
the press on the morning of George's death, summed up not
only his own feelings and those of others who knew George
intimately, but those of every fan who had followed Gipp's
great football career: "George Gipp was the greatest halfback
who has ever represented Notre Dame, and his unquestionable
ability was surpassed by a grit which featured all his work
on the gridiron and was the marvel of his attending physicians. The outstanding feature of his character was a deep
affection for his mother, and in his death I feel a keen
personal loss."

Less than nine hours after Rockne's statement, Gipp's
body was on view at the McGann Funeral Parlor in South
Bend. Lewis McGann recalls that among the thousands of
mourners who came by the parlor to view the body were

many of the city's leading dignitaries, as well as hundreds of darkly attired young women who wept openly as they stood before the bier. Among the mourners were some five hundred of Gipp's fellow students, who filed by the open casket to pay their last respects.

Others stayed away purposely, preferring to remember George as the moleskin-clad superstar who had set their hearts to thumping with his daring, unequalled performances on the football field. Even in death Gipp provoked controversy. Students who saw him as he lay in the open casket were stunned by the effects the ravaging illness had had upon his body. Reports (some highly exaggerated) stated that he had lost as much as eighty pounds during the three weeks he lay ill at St. Joseph's. Some claimed he weighed only eighty pounds at the time of his demise. Teammate Eddie Anderson, the great Gold and Blue end and a favorite target for many of George's passes, viewed the body and was appalled at what he had seen.

Hunk Anderson, who had visited George regularly at the hospital, took issue with subsequent reports of Gipp's purported weight loss. Anderson claimed that George lost at the most thirty pounds. Anderson's contention was confirmed by undertaker Lewis McGann, who prepared the body and who, a little more than a decade later, was to do likewise with the body of Knute Rockne. McGann said that George lost approximately twenty pounds during his stay at St. Joseph's.

On Wednesday, December 15, classes were suspended at Notre Dame in order to permit students to pay their last respects to their celebrated classmate. A requiem high mass in Sacred Heart Church at 8:15 A.M. preceded a solemn procession, which escorted the body on its last trip from the school George had grown to love.

Flags on the Notre Dame campus and the St. Joseph County Court House were at half-mast as the funeral procession, braving the rigors of a blinding snowstorm that had settled over the city earlier that morning, marched along the silent, crowd-lined streets of South Bend en route to the New York Central railroad station. The procession, moving four abreast, formed a line that extended for several blocks. Forming the vanguard was a platoon of police followed by the football team, lined up in signal formation with the position of left halfback vacant. The Monogram Club followed with the entire fourteen-hundred-man student body and the faculty. Behind them came the hearse carrying Gipp's body, flanked on either side by the six men chosen to act as pallbearers. On one side walked Heartly Anderson, Frederic Larson, and Perce Wilcox, the three young men who, thanks to George's unselfish efforts, had followed him to South Bend. They were flanked by Frank Coughlin, Norman Barry, and Joseph Brandy. Three automobiles, carrying members of the immediate family, formed the tail end of the procession.

At 10:28 the body was aboard the baggage car of the train that would carry it to Chicago in the first leg of a trip that would eventually culminate in Calumet. Those final moments at South Bend's New York Central station were vividly captured by a *Tribune* reporter:

> When the first of the escort reached the station, the lines separated and the students bared their heads to the snow as the body of their Gipper went on to its appointed end. Here, where Notre Dame could do no more for its wonder man, the procession waited. As the Chicago train arrived the crowd moved forward toward the casket, which was being prepared to enter the baggage car. A blanket of flowers on which the Notre Dame monogram was mounted, the last symbol of the love of the Notre Dame student body, remained atop it, destined to accompany the body to its final resting place.
>
> Telephone poles, baggage trucks, and every point of vantage

at the station were utilized as the casket was elevated to the door of the car. As though by an unspoken command a hat came off here and there, and in a flash the crowd was bare-headed. Silently, with almost defiant faces, the students gazed at the departing form of their idol.

As the students gazed at the "departing form of their idol," the words used by Father O'Hara in his eulogy at the mass in Sacred Heart Church some hours earlier must have crossed the minds of those in attendance. Perhaps the eulogy offered some consolation to those with deep religious faith. After touching lightly on Gipp's relation to the school, Father O'Hara bade his fellows take comfort from the fact that their schoolmate had enjoyed all the blessings of a happy death, that the last hours of George Gipp had been deeply religious hours in which he had met death fearlessly and with great faith in a future life.

The train carrying the body of George Gipp to its final place of rest pulled into the Chicago station at 1:00 P.M. Wednesday. The train was met by a crowd estimated in excess of ten thousand, a silent, curious crowd that suffered the discomfort of below-freezing temperatures to pay a final tribute to the young man few had ever seen in action. When it was learned that there was to be a four-hour lay-over, several spokesmen for the crowd entreated railroad officials to place the body on display. The request was denied them by George's grief-stricken mother.

The train left the frigid Windy City at 5:00 P.M. and, traveling all night, arrived in Calumet at 8:00 A.M. Thursday morning. A silent, tear-filled crowd, rivaling in number the one that had greeted the train in Chicago, was on hand as the big, noisy locomotive rumbled into the little depot. Late-comers were unable to get within three hundred feet of the baggage car that held the body as the people, many of them friends and relatives, pushed forward to watch the grim proceedings.

On Saturday afternoon, December 18, stores in both Laurium and Calumet closed for the day as the funeral of George Gipp was conducted at Light Guard Armory in Calumet, in the past the scene of some of the gayest, liveliest dances held in the region. The Armory had been chosen since it was the one place that afforded the space required to accommodate the immense crowd expected to come to pay its last respects.

Unlike the service held at Sacred Heart Church, the final service for Gipp was conducted in the protestant rite, with ministers from George's mother's and father's churches, J. Connors and L. B. Robertson respectively, officiating. At this service arranged by George's brother Matthew, Frank Coughlin was called upon to deliver the eulogy. Coughlin said, "George Gipp was perhaps the greatest athlete I have ever known. He was a man among men, brilliant and unassuming, and has endeared himself to the heart of every Notre Dame student by his athletic prowess, magnetic personality, keen mind, and his great love for the old school. He will forever be remembered as a friend, a student, an athlete, and a gentleman, for to know him was to love him."

Outside, a snowstorm that had begun on Wednesday continued unabated, its swirling, powdery flakes swept across snow-packed streets by a stinging wind that charged in from ice-laden Lake Superior. Temperatures in the region dropped to a record low.

Grimly, the Notre Dame pallbearers, wearing neither coats nor boots, went about the task of placing the casket on a horse-drawn sled that was to carry it the last six miles of the journey to the Calumet cemetery, where Gipp would be laid to rest. It was a long, arduous trip, and by the time the procession reached its appointed destination the faces of the faithful were a contrasting crimson to the mountain of whiteness that engulfed them.

Matthew Gipp, George's father, stood over the casket and delivered the final words. In a lot that needed a borrowed foot of ground to accommodate him, George Gipp was laid to rest, twenty-five years, nine months, and thirty days from the date of his birth. Interred with him was the contract offered him by the Chicago Cubs. Besides his father and mother he left as survivors the following brothers and sisters: Alexander Gipp of Philadelphia, Matthew Gipp of Kalamazoo, Mrs. Robert E. Martin of Baraga, Michigan, and Dorothy Gipp of Evansville, Indiana.

Several days after Gipp's interrment heavyweight champion Jack Dempsey offered to give Notre Dame the proceeds from a dance held in the Gold Room of Chicago's Congress Hotel by the Chicago Club. In a wire to the school Dempsey suggested that these proceeds could be used to help defray expenses for a proposed Gipp Memorial. Notre Dame, however, rejected the champ's proposal, stating that it had no wish to solicit or accept outside funds for such a project.

In retrospect it seems to have been a bad time for such charitable offers. Less than twenty-four hours before the Dempsey proposal, the Notre Dame Student Activity Committee, after paying the Indiana Electric Company for some three hundred unpaid fares for students who had used the street-car facilities to reach the McGann Funeral Home, set their sights on raising enough money to defray Gipp's funeral and flower expenses. This time it was the Gipp family who refused the help. Matthew Gipp, Sr., as spokesman for the family, said it was not the intention of the family to accept charity.

In death as in life George's actions, quite unintentionally, provoked controversy. It is not surprising that his final purported act, that of becoming a Roman Catholic, should have engendered arguments. The news that he had converted on his deathbed was received by relatives with a deep sense of shock. Later the shock was displaced by utter disbelief. To this day the debate continues as to whether Gipp converted.

Many people have taken it upon themselves to make the very nature of Gipp's death a controversy as well. This is not in the least surprising, considering the relatively tender age at which George died. With the death of any young person the first question that is asked is whether it could possibly have been avoided. In Gipp's case there is only one answer—an emphatic no. We know that everything known to medical science in the treatment of his illness was tried by some of the best doctors in practice during this era. Therefore we can conclude that Gipp's death can in no way be blamed on the neglect or ignorance of his doctors, Notre Dame, or anybody else. Nobody but Gipp himself, if we take into consideration the fact that he had been advised by his family doctor upon his return home from Flint to have his tonsils removed immediately. However, in checking out the reason for Gipp's visit to Dr. Roche, some startling information has been uncovered.

While in Flint, George had been troubled with shortness of breath and swelling of the ankles. After a preliminary examination, Dr. Roche discovered that George's blood pressure was 180/110, an alarmingly high reading for a young man. These symptoms—shortness of breath, pedal edemia, and hypertension—no doubt had been brought on by a case of rheumatic fever during childhood that had gone undetected. At this point the symptoms indicated congestive heart failure, the prognosis for which was extremely poor. This is to say that George Gipp, had he not contracted a streptococcal infection, still had only a very short time to live.

In the weeks that followed Gipp's death, newspapers from

coast to coast were besieged with unsolicited poems written in his memory by readers whose monumental grief at his passing had been mitigated somewhat by sincere, spontaneous attempts at poetic expression. It would take a sizable volume to accommodate just those poems written within a month of Gipp's passing. Following is one of them, which appeared in a later edition of *The Dome*:

> The little town in Michigan
>   Is tucked beneath the snows.
> A norther from Superior
>   Is calling as it blows.
> Full many a hundred yards or more
>   Lie down the village street
> And seem to wait the darting pass
>   Of famous cleated feet.
>
> The mining shafts of Laurium
>   Are goal posts in the gloaming,
> And the tree tops sound a whistle
>   To the copper miners homing.
> A murmur's in the wind today
>   To all the native hearers,
> And whirling gusts from far Canuck
>   Are twenty thousand cheerers.
>
> The game is on! And through the snow
>   The northers sweep and dip.
> The wind is calling signals
>   To its brother halfback, Gipp.
>
> The Indiana prairie lands
>   Are blanketed with snow;
> The golden dome of Notre Dame
>   Re-gilds the sundown glow.
> On the medieval campus,
>   In the early frosty flurry,

Two thousand men are harking
To the wind's uneasy scurry.

A rat-a-tat of flying feet
Is born from Cartier,
Tho' the gridiron now is barren
And the dusk is in the air.
Is it Army, Purple, Georgia?
Is it scores they now remember?
Or classic catches, leaps and runs,
This evening in December?

The game is on! And through the snow
The northers sweep and dip.
The wind is calling signals
To its brother halfback Gipp!

With the passing of time the pens of these sometime poets have stilled, and in their stead have come the recollections of those people—writers, friends, teammates, and opponents —who knew George best. In the final analysis their opinions, stripped of sentimentality and cleverness of phrase, are the ones that must be pondered and evaluated in order to get a true picture of George Gipp, both as a man and as an athlete. After reading much of what has been said of Gipp by these men through the years, it is evident that George has passed this most difficult of tests. For like the poets who came forth to chart a trail for him that would lead to immortality, these men have been kind to Gipp. Following is a sampling of some of their comments.

Hunk Anderson became Rockne's successor at Notre Dame and still later coached in the pro ranks, earning the esteem of the Chicago Bears' George Halas, who called Hunk the greatest line coach who ever lived. Hunk said: "George was without doubt one of the greatest players of all time. The way he could punt, drop kick, and run the ball was more than brilliant. He could run from any point on the field, combining speed and power with a hip twist that made him the most dangerous man I ever saw in action. His play was a technical treat for football connoisseurs of that time—and how he could drift through interference! His magnetic leadership, his genius as an open field runner, his spine-tingling dashes, and his matchless morale endeared him to thousands and made football history. But although a great football hero, he was not the type of athlete who expected everything to be handed him on a golden platter just because he was a star. Gipp was a man, and what he got he earned."

Donald "Chet" Grant, another teammate of Gipp's and the quarterback of the great '21 team, later became an assistant coach at Notre Dame. Later still, as a successful writer, Grant was terse and to the point when he said, "George's most outstanding quality was his poise."

Lawrence "Buck" Shaw was voted the perfect physical specimen in 1920, and his great play on the line for the Fighting Irish led to a successful career as a coach in the professional ranks. Shaw exclaimed, "The Gipper was the greatest! I've seen players who could run better, who could kick better, and who could pass better, but I've never seen an athlete who could do all three things as well. And few, if any, have had Gipp's poise and confidence."

Notre Dame's great end, Roger Kiley, who followed many of his teammates into the ranks of college coaches before settling into a law career, said, "He was the great athlete. He did everything well. He started so fast in the backfield that centers had trouble passing the ball ahead of him. He was a great blocker, although he wasted very little motion, and I would guess his blocking was largely faking and psychological. Defensively, against passes he was a picture; he never took unnecessary steps. He'd often start toward a receiver but make the judgment that the ball was out of reach and stop. His punts were high and never much beyond Eddie and me downfield. As we say in law, he was *sui generis*—in a class by himself."

Glenn Wilhide, the great Army quarterback of 1920, recalled, "I remember Gipp as the first all-around football player I had ever seen and have seen few since his equal. . . . Had he been playing with the pro teams of 1950 and 1960, my opinion is that he would have surpassed all of them in the records he would have put in the books."

Perhaps one of the finest tributes paid Gipp by a non-athlete came from Warren Brown of the *Chicago Herald* and *Examiner*: "I never saw Gipp play football. I had a chance, though I didn't know it until years afterward. For the Tournament of Roses game at Pasadena on New Year's Day 1921, Notre Dame was practically selected to oppose Andy Smith's California team—and Gipp died. I saw California play that game. I saw California trounce Ohio State, the Western Conference champions, 28-0.

"I saw Brick Muller of California's team throw the longest completed forward pass on record. I thought then I had seen everything. I know now I had seen nothing at all. I hadn't seen Gipp of Notre Dame."

In the years that have passed more concrete expressions of the esteem in which George Gipp was held were added to his memory. The finest of these came at the place where he had seen his first sunset.

On August 3, 1934, a Civic Park and monument were dedicated in Gipp's honor at Laurium. The monument, comprised of colored stones collected in the district, is built in a pyramid. A crowd of five thousand gathered in Gipp's honor and watched as his mother cut the ribbon that unveiled the monument and officially dedicated the park, located on the corner of Lake Linden and Tamarack Streets.

The dedicatory address was delivered by Lyman Frimodig, who said, "Gipp displayed qualities that would make him a success in any walk of life. The greatest of these, that which so many try to achieve but fail, is personality. Of them all that was perhaps Gipp's outstanding characteristic. Few men of the country have, or ever will, achieve the goal of an all-time All-American."

The festivities were brought to a close that day with an exhibition game staged between members of the 1919 and 1920 Laurium baseball teams. All had been former teammates of the great athlete. In the stands that day was Gipp's friend Joe Swetish, manager of the 1919 team, who had driven up from Flint to join in the ceremonies. Swetish, it was learned later, watched the proceedings under the duress of painful injuries. On his way to Laurium the co-owner of Flint's popular Olympic Club, driving a brand-new LaSalle, lost control of his car and went off the road near Lawrence. He received medical attention for cuts and bruises about the head and then continued on to Laurium. That was on Thursday. On Saturday he still complained of pain. Several days later he was dead from injuries sustained in the accident. So it was that the man who claimed to have discovered Gipp followed his protégé to the grave some fourteen years later paying homage to his memory.

That same year the George Gipp All-American trophy was placed in competition at Calumet High School. The trophy, originated by Lyman Frimodig and Will Lavers, is a walnut plaque that holds at its center a large bronze plate containing a lifelike engraving of George in a Notre Dame football uniform. The engraving is circumscribed by a short poem:

Famed fields that echoed hostile shouts
Left him undaunted; he had heard
Superior's voice rise higher than the storm.

Grim foemen answering thrust with thrust
Inspired him onward; he had seen
Imprisoned treasure wrested from the rock.

Cold weariness clutching at the heart
Found him prepared; in his homeland
Green banners mock the north wind's icy blast.

Swift flowing time that humbles man
Can not touch deeds; the record stands
To tempt brave feet to climb the lonely heights.

The trophy is awarded annually to the outstanding senior
on the basis of scholarship, athletic ability, and sportsmanship; it is a symbol of honor at the school.

In 1943 a Liberty Ship named after Gipp was launched at
the Richmond Shipyards just outside of San Francisco.
Perhaps the greatest honor came eight years later, however,
when Gipp was named to the College Football Hall of Fame
at Rutgers University. A similar honor followed in 1957 when
he was unanimously elected to the Michigan Hall of Fame
at Detroit.

In evaluating all of the awards and honors bestowed upon
George, one cannot help but feel that they represent an
extraordinary tribute to a young man whose lifetime barely
exceeded twenty-five years, who was denied the opportunity
to attain material wealth or social position, and who died
with scarcely two hundred dollars in his possession—a sum
that represented all the money he had in the world.

Those to whom awards and honors mean little or nothing,
and those who were denied, by age or opportunity, the
chance to see the Gipper in action, must be content to
measure his greatness by the record he left behind. The
record, as the saying goes, speaks for itself.

In his varsity career Gipp compiled a grand total of 4,833 yards: 2,341 rushing, 1,769 passing, 454 in kick-off returns, 217 in punt returns, and 52 on pass interceptions. He ran for 21 touchdowns, threw 7 touchdown passes, and kicked 27 extra points and 1 field goal for a total of 198 points. In 1920, his greatest year, he averaged an incredible 8.11 yards per rush, picking up 827 yards on only 102 carries. More important, his 4,833 yards set a record at Notre Dame that lasted for nearly half a century.

In amassing this incredible record at Notre Dame, George Gipp led his team to a string of twenty straight wins and to two straight Western championships. The 1920 season, which saw Gipp rise to the pinnacle of his football prowess, is the big reason why many students of Notre Dame football say that the team that represented Notre Dame that year was the best in the school's history. Although this statement may provoke controversy in some quarters, there can be no argument that George's brilliant play in the Army game brought Knute Rockne his first national recognition. And George's daring gridiron deeds have been responsible for the succession of stars who have followed him to Notre Dame, as well as for the immense popularity Notre Dame football teams enjoy to this day.

A tribute to the Golden Age of Sports, ushered in with the help of George Gipp, was once paid by Gene Tunney, who enjoyed that age to its fullest. During a luncheon date with Grantland Rice at the Chatham Hotel, the former undefeated heavyweight champion said:

> Life's been good, awfully good to me, Grant. In my trade at the time—prize fighting—there will never be another period like those twenties. . . . There were a lot of first rate competitors. . . . Also, there were millionaire sportsmen around who had a genuine interest in all sports. If you thought you could make your point, those were the days to prove it.

George Gipp was not a prize fighter. And, unlike Gene Tunney, life was not good to him. But there were a lot of good competitors around in the sports in which the Gipper participated. Given the opportunity, Gipp, too, set out to show he had what it took. What more fitting compliment can one bestow upon him other than to say that he made his point?

Index

Anderson, Edward, x, 95, 118, 119, 131, 155, 158, 178, 181, 196
Anderson, Heartly William "Hunk," ix, 46, 74, 76, 77, 87–92, 95, 98–100, 110, 118, 121, 123, 125, 135, 136, 138, 155, 160, 161, 163, 183, 189, 196, 197, 203
Andrews, Frank "Bodie," 68, 76

Bahan, Leonard "Pete," x, 68, 93, 95, 98, 118, 123, 129, 138, 140–142, 149, 150
Ballmer, Perry, 141, 142, 150, 151
Barry, Norman, x, 66, 100, 155, 157, 158, 167, 177, 178, 182, 197
Bergman, Arthur "Dutch," x, 68, 118, 121, 123, 125, 126
Brandy, Joe, 71, 72, 76, 117, 155, 156, 158, 160, 165, 167, 177, 178, 197
Burns, Father James A., 134–139, 195

Calnon, Mike, 104–107, 110, 129
Camp, Walter, 1, 187, 188
Campbell, Archie R., ix, 143, 148

Cavanaugh, Father John W., 48, 49, 77, 110, 111, 134
Cobb, Tyrus Raymond "Ty," 10, 35, 114, 115
Coughlin, Frank, 117, 118, 123, 127, 128, 155, 160, 167, 178, 197, 199
Cuyler, Hazen Shirley "Kiki," 143, 145–147

Dayton, Harry, 147, 148, 190
Degree, Cy, 117, 118, 123, 155
Dorais, Gus, 79, 81, 88, 94, 128, 134

Eckersall, Walter, 120, 127, 182
Eichenlaub, Ray, 55

French, Walter, 162–165, 167, 169, 170
Frimodig, Lyman, 26, 28, 29, 32, 33, 182

Gipp, Agnes, née Beltes (paternal grandmother), 16
Gipp, Alexander (brother), 20, 39, 168, 200
Gipp, Antoine (paternal grandfather), 16–18
Gipp, Dorothy "Dolly," 20, 21, 59, 175, 187, 200

211

Gipp, Isabella, née Taylor
(mother), 19, 20, 187, 189,
191, 192, 195, 198
Gipp, Mrs. Manila, ix
Gipp, Matthew (brother), 20,
59, 187, 199, 200
Gipp, Matthew (father), 16,
18–20, 200
Grant, Donald "Chet," x, 76, 77,
81, 155
Gray, Wilbur T. "Dolly," 38, 39,
65, 91

Haggerty, Father Pat, 190–192
Halas, Walter, 154, 188
Harper, Jesse, 47–49, 55–57, 62,
66–69, 71, 73, 77–82, 93–95
Hayes, Dave, 68, 76, 117, 155
Hogan, Paul, 29, 38, 39, 161
Hull, George, 104–107, 110,
128–130, 183, 189

Iris, 133, 150, 161, 175, 189

Kessler, Gene, 139, 173, 175,
183
Kiley, Roger, x, 4, 10, 92, 93,
155, 156, 165, 167, 178
Kirk, Bernie, 95, 99, 118, 126,
138, 156
Kline, Merv, 65, 66, 113, 114

Lardner, Ring, 6, 164
Larson, Frederic "Ojay," 22, 30,
88, 91, 92, 95, 98, 100, 118,
152, 153, 155, 159, 160, 166,
178, 197

MacArthur, Douglas, 137
Mack, Connie, 143, 163
Madigan, Edward "Slip," 69, 70,
76, 117, 118, 125
Malone, Grover, 117, 125, 180
Marks, Jack, 69, 80, 94
Mehre, Harry, x, 93, 94, 155
Miller, Walter, x, 51, 67, 68, 76,
117, 118, 124, 125
Mohardt, Johnny, 100, 155, 159,
165, 167, 170, 177, 178, 181,
184
Mohn, Bill, 95, 99, 118
Moore, Elwyn M., 129, 131

Oliphant, Elmer Q., 56, 57, 71,
73, 74

Rice, Grantland, 5, 6, 82, 90,
164, 168
Rockne, Knute Kenneth, 3, 4,
6–10, 12, 45, 46, 48, 50,
52–57, 62, 66, 67, 69, 77–88,
91, 93, 94, 96–98, 104,
117–120, 124, 126, 128, 129,
131, 135–137, 154, 156, 157,
160, 161, 163–167, 174, 176,
179–181, 183, 184, 186, 188,
189, 191, 195, 196, 203
Rydzewski, Frank, x, 67–70, 73,
76, 106

Savinni, Joe, 36, 61, 87, 88, 115,
116, 146
Shaw, Lawrence "Buck," x, 155,
157, 172
Smith, Maurice "Clipper," x, 66,
70, 73, 95, 99, 118, 123, 138,
155, 160
Sorin, Father Edward, 41, 43,
47, 48
Stagg, Amos Alonzo, 69, 94
Stine, Rollo, 95, 118
Strome, Forrest "Dutch," 60,
119
Swanson, Clarence, 121, 156,
158, 159
Swetish, Joe, 112, 113, 116,
139–141, 145, 189, 190

Taylor, Alexander (maternal
grandfather), 20
Taylor, Catherine, née
McInerne (maternal
grandmother), 20
Taylor, Mrs. Dorothy Gipp, ix
Thomson, John, 60, 120
Tobola, Ed, ix, 64

Ward, Arch, 131, 134, 154, 159
Warner, Pop, 137
Wilcox, Perce, 117, 197
Wynne, Chet "Chetter," 100,
155, 157, 158, 164, 167, 168,
178, 179

9